T0077483

Ever wonder why life on earth is so plagued with trouble?
It's because our planet and its inhabitants are under...

THE
CURSE

But there is a Remedy!

Sam Mason

InspiringVoices®

Copyright © 2021 Sam Mason.

All rights reserved. No part of this book may be used or reproduced by any means, graphic, electronic, or mechanical, including photocopying, recording, taping or by any information storage retrieval system without the written permission of the author except in the case of brief quotations embodied in critical articles and reviews.

Inspiring Voices books may be ordered through booksellers or by contacting:

Inspiring Voices
1663 Liberty Drive
Bloomington, IN 47403
www.inspiringvoices.com
844-686-9605

Because of the dynamic nature of the Internet, any web addresses or links contained in this book may have changed since publication and may no longer be valid. The views expressed in this work are solely those of the author and do not necessarily reflect the views of the publisher, and the publisher hereby disclaims any responsibility for them.

All Scripture quotations, unless otherwise indicated, are taken from the Holy Bible, New International Version®, NIV®. Copyright ©1973, 1978, 1984, 2011 by Biblica, Inc.® Used by permission of Zondervan. All rights reserved worldwide. www.zondervan.com The "NIV" and "New International Version" are trademarks registered in the United States Patent and Trademark Office by Biblica, Inc.®

Scripture quotations marked (NASB) taken from the (NASB®) New American Standard Bible®, Copyright © 1960, 1971, 1977, 1995, 2020 by The Lockman Foundation. Used by permission. All rights reserved. www.lockman.org

ISBN: 978-1-4624-1329-4 (sc)
ISBN: 978-1-4624-1330-0 (e)

Library of Congress Control Number: 2021909230

Print information available on the last page.

Inspiring Voices rev. date: 06/01/2021

CONTENTS

Introduction vii
Preface xi
Appreciation xiii

Chapter 1 Paradise Lost 1
Chapter 2 The Curse Falls 17
Chapter 3 A Planet Transformed 37
Chapter 4 The Worldwide Flood 59
Chapter 5 The Post-Flood World 83
Chapter 6 Two Covenants 107
Chapter 7 The Promised Offspring 131
Chapter 8 The Curse Lifted 155

Conclusion 181
Recommended Further Reading 185

INTRODUCTION

All of us have at some point been disillusioned with life on this planet. For some, our cynicism has arisen from a deep personal hurt which has convinced us that life is unfair. For others of us, profound doubts have grown out of years of broader disappointment. We've seen widespread hatred, greed, injustice, violence, disaster, destruction, suffering, disease, poverty, and death. We wonder why it must be this way. Our disenchantment may have its roots in a painful childhood, or it may have developed during adult years. It might have faded with a return to happier times, or clung to us like the burrs of the wild… our attempts to remove it only resulting in more pain. However unique the individual journeys, each has led at one time or another to the same philosophical destination: a universal sense that *all is not right* with the world.

If life itself produces a certain feeling of futility, where can we go to understand why it is so? And more importantly, is there a solution to this predicament? I'm convinced that the answers to these two vital questions are to be found in the best-selling book of all time: the Bible. While not every detail is provided there, in it we clearly discover the essential truths of our existence. There the dark, mysterious cloak that veils life's essence is unraveled.

Despite some apparent contradictions uncovered in a cursory read, through a deeper more intensive study over time, I've discovered the Bible to be a volume amazingly consistent with itself, as well as with real history and true science. Such consistency within its pages is especially compelling when you realize that the Bible is a compilation of 66 separate books penned by more than 30 men of diverse backgrounds over a period of at least 15 centuries. I challenge you to seriously consider this book, and in so doing discover the Bible's reliability for yourself.

The treasures of truth in the work that follows, were excavated through decades of personal reading, study, research, and investigation in the resources of history, science, and Scripture. In the area of Scripture, that effort has been aided greatly by countless godly men and women whose lives, ministries, and writings have touched mine. I've done my best to avoid imposing my own ideas and/or opinions on the Word of God, depending as much as possible upon a scholarly approach to its study. Above all I've prayerfully sought the illumination of the Spirit of God. This is not to assert that my book is infallible. But I am confident that its essential premises are sound. I also would never suggest that I've exhausted the subject on which I've chosen to write. There is far more information to share on this topic than I've chosen to include in this volume.

My method of dealing with this subject will be to present the pertinent truths of Scripture, and the associated facts of history and science*, along with aspects of our common personal life experiences. At times I'll engage in some speculative extrapolation on that data in order to fill in the gaps, and as much as possible, connect the dots.

Although such speculation will be logical and reasonable, distinction will be made between fact and conjecture. Some of these suppositions will only suggest possible implications of the truth or explanations of the facts. Others will lead to virtually irresistible conclusions, which, while requiring some measure of faith, will be rational and intellectually honest deductions. For many of you, this educational expedition will be revolutionary and eye opening. My hope and prayer is that this book will help you understand why the world is like it is, and offer you the joy of discovering the way out of our dilemma.

*It's critical at the outset for me to make a distinction between scientific *fact* and scientific *theory*. Facts are irrefutable conclusions based upon clear empirical evidence and supported by the consistent results of carefully designed repeatable experiments. Theory is supposition offering a possible interpretation of known facts. Unfortunately, frequently the anti-supernatural bias of the dominant segment of the modern scientific community controls public perception of science. They often proclaim as *fact*, that which upon careful unbiased consideration, will be determined to actually be only *theory...* sometimes even downright *faulty theory*.

PREFACE

This book is intended to deal primarily with a spiritual truth which explains why life on earth is not the utopia we might all wish it were, and reveal how a way has been made for things to be set right. In that respect my presentation is philosophical in nature. However; I feel it's important that in some considerable measure I demonstrate the relevance of this spiritual truth to history, science, and real life. That requires a certain amount of technical information. In such portions of the book I've tried to provide just enough data to make the case for these connections, without becoming too detailed. This approach has demanded that I leave out much information which may be of interest to some readers. For those who would like to pursue those topics further, I've included a valuable list of a few other books which deal with these subjects more in depth. You'll find it at the back of this volume under the heading: "Recommended Further Reading."

APPRECIATION

I wish to offer my gratitude to a number of people who have contributed in some way to the writing of this book.

I begin my thanks with a pair of acquaintances: Ian T. Taylor and Dr. Carl E. Baugh. These men are highly respected experts in the field of creation science. Both are authors, lecturers, and hosts - respectively of radio and television programs. I met them through my years in Christian broadcasting. Though I felt compelled to write this book, I approached the task with considerable trepidation, since I had never before authored one. Both Mr. Taylor and Dr. Baugh encouraged me and offered important insights and advice.

I'm grateful to Dr. Dennis Swift, who was kind enough to send me information about the obsidian scalpel in his personal collection of ancient artifacts, allowing me to make reference to it in this book.

I also want to express my appreciation to a number of people who, at my request, proof-read and critiqued my manuscript, helping me to improve it through further suggested revisions. Dr. Floyd Jones was recommended to me by Dr. Baugh. As an expert in both theology and science, his comments were especially instructive and encouraging. Though I have never met him face to face, our limited correspondence has allowed our spirits to bond, and I now consider him a friend. Others who proof-read various drafts of this book and offered valuable input are my good friends Matt and Jeanmarie Elsner, Patty Lauler, and Joseph and Cindy Hall, as well as my youngest daughter, Nicole Ashburn, and my daughter-in-law, Sarah Mason. Lastly, I thank my dear wife, Carol, who not only proofed my work, but supported me in other ways during this effort, enduring patiently with me a difficult personal ordeal which accompanied this undertaking.

CHAPTER 1

Paradise Lost

The glimpse of it we're afforded in the Bible is fleeting. We can't even determine the duration of its relatively brief existence. Our reading of the few sentences in Holy Scripture devoted to it's description leaves us with questions we hardly have time to articulate. Some of those questions may even be unanswerable on this side of eternity. Yet the image created in our minds is appealing enough to engender a powerful inner longing, akin to homesickness. I speak of the Garden of Eden, also referred to as Paradise.

It seems the longer we live, the deeper Paradise tugs on our spirits. Something about this present world seems profoundly awry. When pondered, the data we've accumulated from the vast sources of this information age, and from our own personal life experiences, just "doesn't compute." Some indefinable essential is missing. Why is life not as it seems it should be? We long for an existence that makes sense, and a life that brings fulfillment. What's wrong with the world?

We all search for some means of understanding

this dilemma, of reconciling *what the world is,* with *what it should be.* Many seek the answers in science or philosophy. While those disciplines may provide clues to solving this puzzle, there is only one ultimate source of the clarity we long for: the Creator Himself. And He has chosen to reveal the truth primarily through His Word: the Bible. Only the Scriptures adequately explain the mystery of life.

So where do we commence these discoveries? The obvious place is the beginning, the first book of the Bible: Genesis. The word "Genesis" is derived from a Greek (the language of the New Testament) word meaning "origin" or "beginning." The Hebrew (the language of the Old Testament) title for this book is taken from the first word of its text, which translated into English is the phrase familiar to all Bible readers: "In the beginning." If we want to solve the riddle of the present, we must look to the past, we must go back to the beginning.

Our world began when God *created* the heavens and the earth. The universe as we know it came into existence when *He* made it. Let me make it clear at this point that I am unabashedly a *creationist.* In other words, I do not believe that the universe is self-existent or that life on the earth simply *evolved* from inanimate materials through chance and time. I'm convinced that the universe and life itself are the products of intelligent design, *created* by God. I won't take the time here to expand on the many reasons why I believe so. That's not the purpose of this book. Suffice it for now to say that my belief in intelligent design is a matter of logic and reason.

Also, I further believe that the Genesis account of the origin of the universe and life on earth is accurate and literal. These latter convictions stem from reason *and* faith. As you read through the ensuing chapters, the consistency of the Bible with the historical and scientific evidence, and contemporary conditions on earth (including the sad state of humanity) should become a powerful witness to the veracity of the Scriptures.

Another indication of the authenticity of the biblical account of creation is the common essential elements it shares with other ancient accounts of creation, particularly with the aspects of those accounts dealing with the formation of humans. From the Middle East to Asia and the lands of the southern hemisphere, these stories bear striking similarities to that given in the first two chapters of Genesis. Version after version refers to a god who forms mankind from dust and/or clay, and imparts life from himself.

While some may dismiss the striking similarities of these accounts by speculating that such myths and legends simply have some universal ancient source, I find that very anticipation of a common starting place to be a testimony to the authenticity of *the Scriptural record.* I would argue that the documentation of creation written in the Bible is at the core of all these other creation stories. I'm convinced the Genesis account was dictated by God to Moses, and is therefore fully accurate. The other accounts were likely passed down orally (and later in written form) by fallen humanity from generation to generation, corrupting the facts of the divine narrative with their own revisions. Some essence of truth is there, but inaccuracy has been introduced and multiplied over the course of time.

So what clues to the causes of the present condition of

our world do we find in the opening chapters of Genesis? Did God purposely create a planet rife with all manner of incurable ills? Did He make a design error that eventually led to these terrible flaws? The first part of the answer is that God made everything *good*. At the close of each of the 6 days of creation, God declared of what He had made that day that it was *good*. At the end of the sixth and final day, Genesis 1:31 records: "God saw all that He had made [the entire universe]*, and it was *very good*." The Hebrew word for "good" used in describing this condition, is an adjective which denotes good in every sense of the word. It means: favorable, festive, pleasant, delightful, right, and best. God did not create a world full of trouble and woes. The universe in general, the earth in particular, and the Garden of Eden most specifically, were all "*very* good!" In fact, the Hebrew word "Eden" means "pleasure" or "delight."

The name Paradise is aptly descriptive of this environment. Everything in creation was in its proper place and functioning for good, as God had intended. There was daytime for enjoyment of activities, bathed in the warm glow of the sunshine. There were nights for rest, its darker skies sparkling with the romantic radiance of the moon and stars. The seas and the land presented a diverse panorama of beauty in every direction, and served as homes for every living thing. There were fascinating varieties of plants and animals in which to take pleasure, each with its own unique appeal. God had provided every kind of life with what it needed to flourish. And all of these life forms lived in perfect harmony with one another... including mankind, which was given authority from God to "rule over" (Genesis 1:26) all of the rest. In that regard, humans had been made the Lord's special representatives in this newly created world.

Nowhere in the universe was the beauty and harmony of creation more evident than in the Garden of Eden. I've viewed many naturally majestic vistas. I've visited some lovely man-made gardens. I've seen photographic and television images of the impeccably landscaped grounds of some of the most renowned estates on earth. Yet these images can only start to suggest the magnificence of the Garden of Eden. It was planted by the Master Designer. It featured "...all kinds of trees... that were pleasing to the eye and good for food." (Genesis 2:9) A primary river originated in this garden, flowed through it, was a major water source, and enhanced its ambiance of peace and beauty. Having fashioned this ultimate paradise, God placed the first human beings there. They were to call it home, and "to work it and take care of it." (Genesis 2:15) Its precise location is unknown, but it was likely situated in the Middle East, somewhere near the flood plain of the Tigris and Euphrates Rivers. (Genesis 2:14)

The most delightful aspect of this environment was the precious fellowship those first human beings enjoyed with their Creator. The sense of this beautiful primordial relationship between God and man is conveyed most graphically in these words from Genesis 3:8: "Then the man and his wife heard the sound [or voice]* of the LORD God as He was walking in the garden in the cool of the day..." That the experience described here was not an isolated one, is evident by the fact that the context shows the man and the woman recognized this "sound" as being the presence of the Lord. Recognition generally flows from repetition. The walks God took through the garden in the cool of the day were apparently common. And they were a demonstration of His love for these humans.

Adam and Eve were the apex of God's creation, made, as Genesis 1:27 tells us, "…in his own image." He regularly visited them and fellowshipped intimately with them on *their* level. The image presented here is of a degree of human familiarity with the Lord that we can hardly imagine. Some of us have had a small taste of the Divine presence. And may I say from personal experience, once you've encountered it nothing else in life can ever quite compare. Yet whatever Divine fellowship we may have experienced in this present realm, is shallow compared to the unencumbered intimacy with God enjoyed by Adam and Eve.

The Apostle Paul wrote to the church in the ancient city of Corinth about the companionship of God's Holy Spirit that is given to every true believer as a foretaste of that *fullness* of His presence which will come in a new realm to be entered after we die. He then went on to describe the restrictions of this present life in II Corinthians 5:6: "Therefore we… know that as long as we are at home in the body we are away from the Lord." The current condition of earth and everything in it, places limits on how much of the Lord's presence we can receive in this sad era which lingers between Eden and eternity. The first man and woman experienced living on planet earth as God had intended it to be from the beginning. This was life under the *unhindered blessing* of the Lord, a life that was never meant to be terminated… a life without end!

It may be hard for us to conceive of such a perfect environment. We've never personally experienced it. The bulk of human history, religious and secular, bears little or no resemblance to conditions like those in the Garden of Eden. What has been displayed for us is a world marred by so very much that is amiss. Though we may find this Paradise in the opening chapters of Genesis marvelously appealing, it's blissful state is so foreign to us that the idea that it ever existed resists credibility. The principles of life and nature under which we've lived, challenge its reality. We've inhabited this fallen world so long that its perversions may seem normal, and make the Garden of Eden appear like an absurd fairy tale. Yet this inherent skepticism cannot purge history of the *fact* that this earth was once *favorable, festive, pleasant, delightful, right, and best.* Many of the laws of nature were very different back then... a fact which current conditions on earth make difficult to accept.

So what happened to cause this world to fall from such idyllic beginnings? It was **cursed***!* And this curse was the direct consequence of **sin**. These two words are keys to understanding why life on this planet falls so far short of ideal. In the remainder of this chapter we'll define sin. In the next, we'll explain the curse.

Both the Hebrew and Greek words translated "sin" in the Bible have the same root meaning: "missing the mark." From the beginning God has established a mark, target, or ideal for mankind to hit. Falling short of this objective is sin. God's ideal for human beings is for them to live in perfect relationship with Him and each other. Throughout the Scriptures God established tests of man's loyalty and obedience to Him in these relationships. Inevitably such tests involved commands from God to be obeyed by us.

Even those who've never opened a Bible have likely heard of the Ten Commandments. (Exodus 20:1-17) Most of us have at some time actually read them, or heard them enunciated. These commandments were given to Moses by God as basic moral laws which were to be obeyed by His people. Besides this "Decalogue," as the Ten Commandments are sometimes identified, the Lord communicated many other more detailed laws to His people through Moses.

Later, Jewish religious leaders would add extensively to these commands, resulting in multiplied hundreds of laws which they insisted must also be followed in order to please God. To break any of this plethora of minutely precise manmade commands was supposedly sin. This became a burden of obedience so staggering that the apostle Peter, speaking at a council of early Christian leaders during the first century A.D., referred to these laws as "…a yoke that neither we nor our fathers have been able to bear." (Acts 15:10)

By contrast, the first man and woman were presented with a simple standard of obedience to God through a handful of commands. God blessed them, then told them to produce many children, to rule (as His representatives) over the earth and everything in it, and to serve as gardeners in Paradise. These first directives were completely positive and enjoyable. God had made procreation a most pleasurable physical expression of love. And having created humans in His image, He had included His "father's heart" of love for their children as part of their makeup. Being leaders and stewards of the planet entailed satisfying responsibilities and great honor. It included caring for the Garden and enjoying its delightful fruit.

Then He instructed them specifically as to what they should eat. Even this final directive was predominately positive. They were given the fruit of "every seed-bearing plant on the face of the whole earth" as food. (Genesis 1:29) Two trees in the middle of the Garden of Eden were mentioned by name: the tree of life and the tree of the knowledge of good and evil. The only negative command Adam and Eve were issued was "you must not eat from the *tree of the knowledge of good and evil.*" (Genesis 2:17) Just this one divine *prohibition* was placed upon them. They were even provided a logical reason for this ban: "...when you eat of it you will surely die." (Genesis 2:17) We can hardly imagine a test of loyalty and obedience to God simpler than that given to the parents of all mankind. These were pleasant obligations, and just a single "*do not.*"

With such a wonderful environment and very simple and agreeable duties, what could possibly have precipitated man's fall into sin? It seems that Adam and Eve would have known total contentment. Well, those first *humans* may have been content, but an as yet unknown *sinister life form* lurking in the shadows was not! And he was about to sow the seeds of discontent. Enter "the devil," also commonly known as Satan, and occasionally referred to as Lucifer, Beelzebub, and other lesser known names and titles. This trespasser arrived in Paradise in the form of a serpent, or snake.

Genesis 3:1 tells us that the serpent was "more crafty than any of the wild animals the LORD God had made." Ancients identified the snake with wisdom, possibly because of their cunning way of hunting and attacking prey. Jesus Himself acknowledged this clever ability in Matthew 10:16 when He instructed His disciples to "be as shrewd as snakes." Significantly, the trait of "craftiness," which was a characteristic of the snake, is of itself morally neutral. It can be used for good or evil purposes. In this case, the serpent's craftiness was used to beguile mankind into sin and rebellion against their Maker. Thus, in addition to having been considered symbols of wisdom, snakes have also eventually come to be frequently identified with sin and evil.

But this snake was not acting strictly on its own. The devil was using it, probably through "possessing" it, that is, entering into its body and taking control of it. One indication of this is that the serpent *spoke* to Eve. In spite of its cunning, I see no reason to expect that the snake ever had native ability to speak to humans. The only other incidence in Scripture (Numbers 22:21-35) of an animal speaking to a human being, is a case where a supernatural power from God was enabling it (a donkey) to speak for divine supernatural objectives. In the episode before us, the supernatural ability for the serpent to speak came from the devil. This association of the snake with Satan in the first book of the Bible, is confirmed by the last book of the Bible. Both Revelation 12:9 and 20:2 refer to Satan as "...*that ancient serpent*." The use of the adjective "that" singles out a specific serpent. And the use of the adjective "ancient" points to the first serpent ever mentioned in history: the one in this story of temptation and sin in the Garden of Eden.

Who is the devil? The answer could become an entire book in itself, but for the purposes of this study my explanation will be limited. Let me give you the most basic information about Satan. His name means "adversary or accuser, one who lies in wait." He is seen repeatedly in this role throughout Scriptures, where he opposes and accuses God and His people. He was originally created as an angel, but he became discontented with his position *under* God, and wanted to exalt himself *above* God. At some point the devil yielded to the sin of pride, and in his seditious ambition led a rebellion against the Lord. He was defeated and with one-third of the angels who had joined his revolt, was cast out of heaven. In Luke 10:18 Christ told His disciples that He had witnessed this ancient event. Satan has powers far greater than those of humans, but inferior to those of God.

It is in this ancient role of adversary and accuser that he approached Eve through the serpent, sowing his own discontent into the life of human beings. His objective was to oppose and displace the dominion of God and God's representatives: Adam and Eve. His strategy was to falsely accuse God, and present his own lies as the alternative to God's truth. He began by planting doubt and confusion in the mind of Eve. "Did God *really* say, 'You must not eat from any tree in the Garden?'" (Genesis 3:1) In so doing, He misstated the Lord's command, expanding it to apply to *all* the trees. Satan questioned God's veracity, and Eve's knowledge of the truth.

Her response at first was to correct the devil's misrepresentation of God's command. She pointed out that the Lord had given them permission to eat fruit from all the garden trees except one. But then she apparently added error by saying that God had not only prohibited *eating* of the tree of the knowledge of good and evil, but had told them "...you must not *touch* it, or you will die." (Genesis 3:3) Since there is no record of God prohibiting *touching* this tree, we might presume that at some point either Adam, Eve, or both, introduced this error into the response to the devil's query. This portion of the conversation represents a pattern of interaction between the devil and humans which has continued in the millennia since then. Satan introduces doubt and confusion, and those not well-grounded in divine truth often add their own error to the muddle.

The serpent's subsequent assertion escalated the level of dialogue from that of introducing *doubt,* to engaging in outright *denial* of the truth. "You will *not* surely die," he claimed. (Genesis 3:4) Emboldened by his success in producing ambiguity and uncertainty, the devil now challenged God's very integrity by in essence calling Him a liar! Then he went on to malign God's motives, suggesting that his decree had been self-serving. He continued, "For God knows that when you eat of it your eyes will be opened, and you will be like God, knowing good and evil." (Genesis 3:5)

This part of his argument was not an outright lie, but a distortion of the truth. This also is part of the devil's strategy. A kernel of truth wrapped in a falsehood often lends enough pseudo-authority to this huckster's persona to enable him to sell the whole package. Adam and Eve would soon become the first of Satan's paying customers. And they would quickly discover that becoming like God in "knowing good and evil" would not translate into becoming like God in *holiness, authority, and power.*

Eve's next mistake was to entertain a dangerous emotional guest. Godly *contentment* was about to give way to ungodly *lust.* Lust is a "strong desire." In Scripture it's used predominately of strong desire for *wrong* things. A simple explanation of how it works in our lives is found in James 1:13-15: "When tempted, no one should say, 'God is tempting me.' For God cannot be tempted by evil, nor does He tempt anyone; but each one is tempted when, by his own evil desire [lust]*, he is dragged away and enticed. Then, after desire has conceived, it gives birth to sin; and sin, when it is full-grown, gives birth to death." The fact that lust *conceives,* implies that an intimate intercourse of some kind has taken place between the individual and lust. The child of this union is *sin,* and the grandchild is *death.* This was to be the tragic result of Eve's liaison with lust.

She began by simply looking at the forbidden fruit. She and Adam had never needed it before. Their life with God in paradise had been wonderful and fulfilling. But now, just looking at it increased her desire for it. Eve saw that it "was good for food and pleasing to the eye, and also desirable for gaining wisdom." Then her tryst with lust produced its inevitable offspring. She took the fruit of the tree of the knowledge of good and evil and ate some. She gave some to Adam, who also ate it. **Sin** had entered paradise.

Adam and Eve's disobedience to the Lord's single "do not" command was mankind's first sin. Yet their specific disobedience was mere outward evidence of what is at the core of sin: idolatry. On the surface, sin is disobedience to God's commands. At its heart, sin is missing the mark of the perfect relationship He desires to have with us. That relationship requires that God be who He is, and we be who we are. *God must be God and we must be His children!* The nucleus of sin is making anyone (including ourselves) or anything else... other than the Lord Himself... God. And that, my friends, is idolatry. It had been the original sin of the devil, and it became the original sin of mankind.

When the divine order of things is disrupted, that is sin. And when sin comes into our existence, it brings consequences. The first of those consequences came in the form of lost innocence for Adam and Eve. What had been good and natural in their lives before sin... nakedness... became shameful in its aftermath. They fashioned primitive clothing for themselves by sewing fig leaves together, but it was equivalent to the proverbial closing of the barn door after the cows have left. The damage was done. The precious gift of innocence had been squandered.

I'm reminded of a greeting card I once saw. The cover featured a cartoon image of an elderly man and woman sitting together on a park bench. One says to the other, "Remember how when we were children we couldn't wait to grow up?" Upon opening the card, this brief conversation concludes with the rhetorical question, "How stupid was that?" The old saying is true. We usually don't appreciate what we have until it's gone. Humanity's first couple had bought into the deception that ultimate fulfillment was to be found in "growing up" into gods. Sin had pounced upon them as suddenly as a tiger, and stripped them naked.

They soon realized they'd been better off before they ate of the forbidden fruit. The beauty and innocence of their original relationship with God was lost. The initial indication of this came when, for the first time, Adam and Eve *hid* from the presence of God. To those who enjoy an intimate bond with the Lord, His presence is welcome. But in the hearts of those whose relationship with Him has been broken by sin, that same presence elicits fear. In fact, Genesis 3:10 records the first mention of fear in the history of the world. Imagine a life without fear. That's what unspoiled Eden offered in the beginning. Once, "the sound of the LORD God as He was walking in the garden in the cool of the day" (Genesis 3:8) was an overture to sweet fellowship with their Creator. Now it had become a prelude to judgment... a judgment from which they tried unsuccessfully to hide.

Evasive action by the man and his wife was futile. God sought them out and began asking questions. It's important here to understand that the Lord does not ask us questions because He doesn't know the answers and needs us to tell Him. He asks questions to provide us an opportunity to be honest with ourselves and with Him. "Where are you?" (Genesis 3:9) the Creator called to the man. Adam answered "I heard You in the garden and I was afraid because I was naked; so I hid." (Genesis 3:10) Next, God queried, "Who told you that you were naked? Have you eaten from the tree that I commanded you not to eat from?" (Genesis 3:11)

Then began the blame game. Adam started by essentially faulting God first, then the woman God had given him. "The woman *you* put here with me - *she* gave me some fruit from the tree, and I ate it." (Genesis 3:12) When the Lord turned His interrogation to the woman, Eve followed suit, "The serpent deceived me and I ate." (Genesis 3:13) According to Adam it wasn't his fault, it was Eve's fault for leading him into sin, *and* it was even God's fault for making Eve in the first place. But then again, according to Eve it wasn't really her fault either, since the serpent had led her into unbelief and disobedience with his lies. And maybe, like her man, Eve was also implying that it was the Creator's fault, since *He* had made the snake.

It's been said that success has many parents while failure is an orphan. The same can be said for righteousness and sin. Not much has changed in the centuries since the initial fall of mankind. If anything has changed, perhaps it's that society has become even more adept at avoiding responsibility for its bad behavior. Contemporary American culture in particular has excelled in its efforts to avoid personal accountability. We have become a nation of victims. Responsibility for our faults and failures is repeatedly placed upon other individuals, groups, or circumstances. But God's justice is not based upon contemporary American culture. Its foundation is the unchanging principles of His timeless truth. In the court of His final judgment, "each one of us will give an account of *himself* to God." (Romans 14:12)

As we'll discover in the next chapter, no one who participated in the original fall of man would be able to shirk responsibility for sin, or avoid the penalties. The first man and woman were about to be driven from Paradise, and the full blessing of God was soon to yield to a powerful, sweeping curse that was going to affect the whole planet!

*Not in the original text. Added by the author for clarification.

CHAPTER 2

The Curse Falls

The curse that's recorded in Genesis chapter 3 is the most momentous in human history. But it is not the only curse mentioned in the Bible. The Scriptures tell of numerous curses, potential curses, and their causes. The essential cause of biblical curses is disobedience to God. As we discovered in the previous chapter, the Creator's original intent for mankind and his environment was to bless them. That continues to be His desire. But a curse falls when we rebel and disobey. And a curse does not come without a warning from God.

He warned Adam and Eve that eating the fruit of the tree of the knowledge of good and evil would bring death. When He later dictated the Ten Commandments to Moses in Exodus chapter 20, those and further divine regulations carried with them promises of rewards for obedience, and punishments for disobedience. In Deuteronomy chapter 28, shortly before his death, Moses and the priests communicated to God's chosen people a detailed exposition of the blessings that would flow as a result of following God's law, and the curses that would fall in response to defiance of that same law. There are many more passages throughout the Word of God relating to curses. And always the choice between blessing or curse is left to us.

The curse that followed Adam and Eve's initial sin is the most consequential curse ever to have been pronounced. Its uniqueness lies in the fact that it was the *first* curse and the *most pervasive* curse in the annals of this planet. Though it was directed primarily at Adam, Eve, and the serpent, its long arm of impact and cold hand of death would reach far beyond the time and space occupied by the rebellious trio who opened the gate for it. It will for all time be spoken of as **the** curse.

Before going any further, let me clarify what is meant by a curse… specifically a *divine* curse. A divine curse is a pronouncement of negative consequences upon a person or persons, place, or thing. Only God has full authority to curse. As I said, His curses are generally brought down by rebellion against Him and His commands. On the other hand, a human curse is less a *pronouncement*, than a *wish* or *appeal* to a higher power for negative consequences upon someone. God has the power to prevent, or even reverse the curses of men, causing human curses to turn back upon the curser, or turning those curses into blessings for those who have been cursed by man.

A blessing, of course, is the opposite of a curse. A blessing is a pronouncement, wish, or appeal for positive consequences. The Genesis account of creation, and indeed the whole of Scripture, clearly demonstrate that *blessing* is the Lord's first choice for mankind and the earth, with all its creatures. But disobedience to His commands, and insurrection against His authority and plan, inevitably lead to a curse.

Thus, Genesis 3:14 introduces us to that first and most profound curse ever pronounced. Having established the culpability of those involved in the rebellion in Paradise, God proceeded to enunciate the curse that would fall upon the guilty parties. Bear in mind as I recount the results of the curse, that the penalty reaches far beyond the unholy triumvirate directly responsible for the original sin.

The Lord began pronouncing judicial sentences with the snake. It's important to note here that the snake was not the primary culprit. Satan was. But the serpent participated with the devil, and thus bears a measure of the guilt. The Lord revealed a principle in Exodus 21:28-36 which applies to this situation. In those verses He established that if an animal does harm to someone, and the animal's owner has contributed in any way to that injury, *both* the animal and its owner must bear responsibility. So God pronounced judgment upon the snake. "Because you have done this, cursed are you above all the livestock and all the wild animals! You will crawl on your belly and you will eat dust all the days of your life. And I will put enmity between you and the woman, and between your offspring and hers; he will crush your head, and you will strike his heel." (Genesis 3:14,15)

It's apparent from God's edict to the snake: "cursed are you *above all the livestock and all the wild animals,*" that every animal came under the curse of sin in some measure. But the serpent was singled out to be cursed more than the rest because of his complicity with the devil. His pivotal role in the fall of mankind produced for him a most terrible consequence, one that has attached to him a sinister stigma for all time. The enmity between the snake and the offspring of woman, and the snake's characteristic of striking at the heels of people, likely accounts in large part for the fact that snakes are among the most hated and feared of earth's creatures.

One of the more common of human phobias is known variously as "snakephobia," "herpetophobia," or "ophidiophobia:" the fear of snakes. Other wild animals we fear, such as lions and wolves, have at least some positive appeal to us as well. They seem to express a kind of strength and nobility. Most of us sense an endearing quality about their cubs and pups. Even some of the snake's fellow reptiles, chameleons and geckos for example, may draw some level of warm feelings from us. But few find anything cuddly or affectionate about a snake. This creature crawls on its belly and strikes at our heels.

The fact that God condemned the snake to crawl on it's belly from that day forward, tells us that its previous mode of locomotion was different. We're not told what that was, but it seems most likely that it had legs. Interestingly, in the year 2000, the American Association for the Advancement of Science reported an amazing discovery at a site in the middle east. Archeologists uncovered the fossil of an ancient snake *with a set of hind legs*. It was suggested by scientists that this finding could overturn the prevailing naturalistic theory that snakes had evolved from earlier water dwelling creatures. But that same finding lends support to the Genesis account of the Lord's curse upon serpents. Did the snake immediately lose its legs, or did they gradually disappear? We cannot answer that question. Nonetheless, the final outcome is that snakes crawl as a result of the curse of God upon them for their part in the first human sin.

In a related edict, God told the snake that it would eat dust all the days of its life. This could be meant literally, in that living and eating so low to the ground may result in snakes consuming more dust with their meals than other animals. Or eating dust could be a symbolic reference to its humiliation. "Eating dust" is an ancient derogatory expression. In Micah 7:17 the Lord compares evil nations to snakes who "will lick dust." In American slang, the hated villain always "bites the dust." And similar expressions are found in other writings, dating as far back as Homer's Iliad, Book II. Perhaps all these phrases find their origin in God's telling the snake he would "eat dust."

The final ingredient of the curse that God pronounced upon the snake, had to do with its relationship with Eve. It was Eve he targeted for deception. Eve became the first human victim of Satan's plot to overthrow God's authority... Eve: the mother of all mankind. And forevermore there was to be enmity between the devil's primeval collaborator, the serpent, and it's descendents; and the woman and her descendents. This deep-seated mutual hostility would for thousands of years be demonstrated through malignant interaction between the two species. The Lord declared to the snake that the woman's offspring "will crush your head, and you will strike his heel." (Genesis 3:15)

An estimated 20,000 people worldwide annually die from snake bites. Yet that number of human fatalities from snake bites pales in comparison to the number of snakes killed by humans each year. Just the various annual rattlesnake roundups in a few southwestern states in the U.S. probably kill that many. Snakes may continue to strike at man's heel, but man continues to crush his head. The once shrewd serpent has been brought low by the curse of original sin. He still stirs fear and brings death to some, but with his abilities diminished and his legs removed, he's relatively easy prey for mankind.

The vulnerability of snakes was demonstrated to me personally in my late teens. For two summers during my Bible school years I labored at my uncle's tree farm. One of the fields we worked was infested with rattlesnakes. In spite of my uncle's assurances to me that over the years none of his workers had ever been bitten, my fear was so great that the first day we pruned trees there I wore two pairs of pants, two pairs of heavy work socks, and goulashes. My sweat-soaked discomfort soon exceeded my fears, and by the second day I dressed normally. In the two seasons I labored in that area, no workers were ever bitten, but a handful of rattlers were easily killed by the workers.

Now, as with many other passages of Scripture, Genesis 3:15 has a double reference. God's pronouncement of the enmity and conflict that would transpire between the offspring of the woman and the snake applied not only *naturally* to the serpent, but *spiritually* to the evil entity who had possessed and used it. And while the Lord's reference to the woman's offspring broadly applies to all humanity, it also points prophetically to Jesus Christ and his followers. This identification is confirmed in the New Testament in Galatians 4:4 where God says "But when the time had fully come, God sent his Son, born of a woman..." The 12th chapter of the book of Revelation also gives a graphic picture of this conflict between the woman's offspring (Jesus, and His followers) and "that ancient serpent," also referred to as the "dragon." (Revelation 12:9) And Romans 16:20 repeats the phraseology of Genesis 3:15 in speaking of the Christian's final victory over the devil: "The God of peace will soon crush Satan under your feet."

The ultimate battle is not between men and snakes, rather it is God versus Satan. Just as Adam and Eve were created to be God's representatives on earth, the snake had figuratively become the devil's representative. The real conflict behind the scenes in the opening verses of Genesis chapter 3 was between God and the devil. Thus, the latter part of the curse against the serpent was to find its greatest fulfillment in the epic battle between the Son of God (Jesus) and Satan. I'll speak of that crucial clash further as this book progresses.

Having pronounced sentence upon the snake, God turned his attention to the next in line: the woman. Eve was the first human being to be recruited into the devil's rebellion against the Creator. She had listened to the serpent's rationale, and in due course chose to believe his lies instead of God's Word. She yielded to her lust for the forbidden fruit, ate some of it, then invited her husband to join in her fateful act of disobedience.

To the woman God said: "I will greatly increase your pains in childbearing; with pain you will give birth to children. Your desire will be for your husband, and he will rule over you." (Genesis 3:16) The curse God pronounced upon her dealt with two areas of her life: childbirth and marriage.

It's interesting that the Lord said He would *greatly increase* the woman's pains in childbirth. The question arises: *Greatly increase* above what? It may be that God had originally designed birth to involve some lower level of discomfort for the woman, and that the curse led Him to very much intensify that pain. However, this appears unlikely to me.

Though the Bible does not specifically tell us so, I don't believe pain had any place in paradise or on the recently created earth. In the establishment of a new heaven and a new earth planned by the Lord for the end of time, as recorded in Revelation chapter 21, God declares "There will be no more... pain..." (Revelation 21:4) That untarnished fresh creation will be dealt with more fully in chapter 8 of this book. But for now let me state that, in my estimation, through the making of a new heaven and earth in the future, God intends to essentially restore the conditions prevalent prior to the fall of man. And these conditions apparently excluded pain. So I don't believe that when God said He would *greatly increase* pain in childbirth, He meant that He would greatly increase it over some degree of childbearing discomfort He had already established for women. I'm persuaded that this *increase* in birth pains reflects a different comparison.

A few years ago, after mentioning this increase in the pain of childbirth during a message I shared as a guest speaker in a church in my area, I was approached by a man who told me he'd worked with animals for many years. He informed me that his experience had clearly demonstrated to him that no other creature endures the agony in childbirth that humans do. I have since confirmed the fact of his observation in a discussion with my veterinarian.

We learned from God's proclamation to the snake that other animals would also be affected by the curse, since the snake was to be cursed "*above all* the livestock and all the wild animals." (Genesis 3:14) I believe that birth pains for earth's creatures are one of the effects of the curse. The increase in the woman's level of pain in childbirth was a multiplication of that relatively minor discomfort to be suffered by other animals giving birth to their young. God did not originally intend for birth be painful. Severe labor pains for humans are a penalty for the first woman's part in the first sin.

Yet the very same event that brings such intense agony to women, also brings them one of life's greatest joys. In John 16:21,22 the Lord Jesus compares this particular pleasure to the delight that would follow the grief that He and His disciples were about to endure at the time of his crucifixion and death. "A woman giving birth to a child has pain because her time has come; but when her baby is born she forgets the anguish because of her joy that a child is born into the world. So with you: Now is your time of grief, but I will see you again and you will rejoice, and no one will take away your joy." Even though the curse would result in much labor pain, God in His mercy intended for that labor pain to usher in much happiness! Few things in life ennoble a woman more than childbirth and child nurture.

The next stage of the curse upon the woman profoundly affected the marriage relationship for all time. The first element of it declared that her desire would be for her husband. Initially, that hardly strikes us as being negative. Yet if it's part of the curse it must be detrimental. There has to be something unusual about this kind of desire on the part of a wife toward her husband. Interestingly, some Bible scholars interpret this "desire" as a wish to dominate her husband. I personally think that God is speaking here of the inordinate level of emotional dependence upon her man that is common among many wives.

This kind of desire is a perversion of the original respect and tender longing God intended for wives to feel toward their husbands. Such exaggerated feelings are a harmful aberration that can trap a woman in a home with a violent, severely abusive man. She can't leave him because she thinks she can't live without him. Frequently she even begins to feel she deserves the abuse. Her *desire is for her husband.* To a great degree, from this inordinate desire for her husband flows the final element of the curse on the woman: "...he will rule over you." (Genesis 3:16)

Starting with the Lord as Supreme Ruler, the various ranks of legitimate authority on earth were instituted by a loving God (Romans 13:1) to be for the benefit of all mankind. (Hebrews 13:17) Remember, the curse itself was the result of Adam and Eve's rebellion against God's direct authority. Paradise was lost to all mankind because of that Satan-inspired revolt. However, when sin poisons God-appointed human authority, benevolent management mutates into tyranny.

While I'm convinced scripturally that the headship of the husband in the marriage relationship was part of God's original creation order, I'm also certain that the curse allowed that perfect design to be perverted at times. Although the corruption of God's design for the husband-wife relationship has been manifested in many ways, perhaps the most common form of that corruption is still that which results from a woman's excessive longing for her husband and a man's selfish overbearing abuse of his authority over his wife. These are consequences of the curse.

Finally, after dealing out sentences to the others, the Lord turned his attention to Adam. As the first human being, he had initially been given authority as God's representative to rule over the earth and all its creatures. He was the first to enjoy sweet fellowship with the Almighty. With the weight of so much responsibility and so many blessings from God resting on his shoulders, Adam had much for which to answer. It was not the serpent God summoned after the seditious act of partaking of the forbidden fruit. It was not the woman to whom his voice beckoned. "But the LORD God called to *the man*, 'Where are you?'" (Genesis 3:9) When God queried Adam about the evil deed, the man cast the blame toward "the woman," whom he observed, "you [God]* put here with me." (Genesis 3:12) But like a boomerang, the blame had returned to the one who had flung it toward his wife and his God. Now the Judge of all men was about to pronounce sentence upon the first man, and through him (as also through his wife), upon all mankind.

The curse that fell upon Adam centered around the earth from which he was made, and over which he had been given responsibility and dominion. God decreed: "Cursed is the ground because of you; through painful toil you will eat of it all the days of your life. It will produce thorns and thistles for you, and you will eat the plants of the field. By the sweat of your brow you will eat your food until you return to the ground, since from it you were taken; for dust you are and to dust you will return." (Genesis 3:17-19)

Until that momentous day, Adam's needs had been supplied by his Creator through his environment... with minimal effort on Adam's part. At this instant came a radical change. So far, through the judgment upon the snake and the woman, sin had taken its toll on Satan, the human race, and the animal kingdom. Now it's tentacles grasped the plant kingdom and the entire planet.

Anyone who has ever labored with lawn or garden has marveled at how hearty weeds are in comparison to the grass, flowers, or vegetables we're trying to grow. Weeds don't need people to plant them… they don't need cultivating… they don't need fertilizing… sometimes it seems they don't even need water! In our frustration we wonder why it is so. Like a multitude of life's troubles, this unhappy reality in the plant world goes back to the curse.

My brother-in-law and I sometimes jokingly say to one another: "This working for a living is for the birds!" But the truth is that it's not for the birds. It's for people. As we saw in chapter one, God planned for man to have a pleasant career in paradise. But that pleasant career became hard labor because of the curse sin brought with it. In our contemporary supermarket world you and I may no longer grow our own food, my friend, but somebody grows it for us. I have great respect for the farmer. Is there anyone who works harder, with less financial return for his long hours than the farmer? And whether literally or figuratively, most of us buy that food with money we've earned through hard work. No matter how you look at it, we still *eat our food by the sweat of our brow.* We can thank Grandpa Adam for that reality. But let's not be too hard on him, since we too, have fallen prey to sin.

And what happens after a lifetime of hard labor? We die. The disturbed perspective which that reality produces in many people was articulated through a rather earthy adage I saw many years ago on a bumper sticker. It read: "You're born, you work, then you die. Life sucks!" The Lord stated it without the crudity and cynicism reflected on the bumper sticker, telling Adam he would work hard for his food until he "returned to the ground." (Genesis 3:19) But the bottom line is still the same. Sin has delivered us over to death.

Ask a thousand people what they fear most, and the number one answer in a landslide will be *death.* We may find a bright spot in most every other aspect of the curse. Our chance of being bitten in the heel by one of those vile snakes is pretty slim, and in the numbers game mankind is winning the war against our ancient reptilian nemesis. Excruciating birth pains conclude with the joy of holding a precious baby in our arms. Even with all the problems replete in the husband/wife relationship, most people still find marriage a desirable arrangement. Along with the bone deep weariness which hard labor generates, a certain amount of satisfaction can also be drawn from it. But it's difficult to find a silver lining in the black cloud of death. By its very definition death brings life to an end and, after all, life is understood to be the most precious gift we possess.

It's obvious that the climax of the curse is death. It was death of which God warned the first humans when he commanded them not to eat of the fruit of the tree of knowledge of good and evil. And it was the sentence of death that concluded the proclamations of the curse of sin. That very day death entered into every cell of Adam's and Eve's bodies. God had created them to live forever. Now the sinister process of death began to slowly consume the very life from their flesh. Scientists tell us that every time a cell in the body divides, a piece of the tail end of each gene, known as a "telomere," breaks off, and the telomere shrinks. The result is the gradual degeneration of the body and its vital functions. When the telomere disappears completely, we die. This process began in our first parents thousands of years ago. It begins in us at birth. We unfortunately, are born to die. This is the end result of the curse.

That all people die only as a result of the curse opens a fascinating topic for conjecture. What if Adam and Eve had not sinned, the curse had never fallen, and all humans continued to live forever? Wouldn't population explosion eventually become a huge problem? With no one ever dying, and births of new people taking place constantly, wouldn't the earth sooner or later become overcrowded? I'm sure that an omniscient (all-knowing) God would have foreseen that budding dilemma.

We can only guess how He would dealt with it. Would He have stopped or restricted human reproduction at some point? I doubt it. Might He have instituted a seniority system whereby those with lengthy enough residence on earth might be promoted to heaven? Maybe. Perhaps He would have enlarged the earth or re-located people to countless earth-like planets throughout His grand universe. The possibilities are many. Whatever the case, an innocent, uncorrupted earth with no death would be a problem with which most of the human race would happily deal. And it would be a problem for which God would have no doubt provided a pleasant solution.

There is yet another kind of death that is worse than the physical death which we've been discussing. *Spiritual death*, too, is a result of the curse. Those who choose to become their own gods, as Adam and Eve did, alienate themselves from the one and only true God: our Creator. Life comes from Him. Not just physical life, but spiritual life. Our spirits are from God, so to be separated from Him is to be spiritually dead. That's why those who want to return to the Lord must be "born again" of the Spirit of God. (John 3:5,6) When we are born again our dormant spirits essentially come back to life through reconciliation with God.

Spiritual death will one day lead to what the Bible calls the *second death*. Those who reject God must not only face physical death, but will one day face an irrevocable second death. The book of Revelation speaks powerfully of this future event. It tells us that the second death is "the lake of fire." Revelation 20:15 says that following the final judgment: "If anyone's name was not found written in the book of life, he was thrown into the lake of fire." The second death is a place of eternal torment, isolated from the loving God who made us and wants to bless us abundantly in the divine order of things. I'll discuss this and other "end time" events further in the final chapter of this book.

How can we avoid this second death? Only through being "born again." Genesis 3:21 lays a foundation for understanding this lone means of escape: "The LORD God made garments of skin for Adam and his wife and clothed them." You may recall that upon realizing their nakedness in the wake of sin, this couple sewed fig leaves together in an attempt to clothe themselves. In their rebellion against God and His command, they had sought to become *like* God with their own total sovereignty. They soon discovered however; that only the real God can make an adequate covering for the moral nakedness that sin reveals.

The Lord made garments of animal skins. This little fact is extremely significant in more than one way. Most importantly, it prefigures God's plan of redemption for mankind. First, though, let's pursue its implications for the animal kingdom. The making of that clothing required the death of animals. Behind the scenes at the fall of man was the first death of any living creature in the history of the planet. It was a tragic moment. Why do I assert that this was the first? While I cannot make an open and shut case, just such an interpretation can easily be extrapolated from what is stated in the Bible.

It is clear that *man* was never meant to die. The first mention of death in the Bible was only as a *possibility*, not an *inevitability*. If Adam and Eve had not disobeyed God, they would have lived forever. And if God never meant for humans to die, there's no reason to expect that He intended animals to die either. In Genesis 2:19,20, we're told that God brought all the animals to the man to be named by him. This brief account ends with the statement: "But for Adam no suitable helper was found." It appears that during this procedure the man and his Maker were keeping their eyes open for an appropriate companion for Adam. None was found, and the Lord subsequently made the woman. A logical question arises: if animals were being considered as potential companions for a man who would never die, would God have been contemplating a *mortal* friend for an *immortal* man? Not likely.

Additionally, evidence supporting the conclusion that animals were not originally subject to death is found in Genesis 1:29, where the Lord told Adam "I give you every seed bearing plant on the face of the whole earth and every tree that has fruit with seed in it. They will be yours for food." The first man was a vegetarian. He had no reason to kill animals. And in the next verse (Genesis 1:30) God gave "...every green plant for food" to the animals. The original creation included no carnivores. Man and animals did not kill and eat one another.

Further, Romans 5:12 establishes that "...sin entered *the world* through one man, and death through sin." The implication is that death entered not just into the life of humans, but into the life of *the whole world.* Similarly, Romans 8:21 states that the *whole creation* was made subject to decay as a result of sin and the curse. Decay speaks of degeneration, which leads to death. In other words, sin brought death not only to man, but to *all creation*, including the animals. Death made its debut on earth with the demise of the animals which were killed to make Adam and Eve's covering of skins.

Death became part of the fabric of the whole earth because of the curse of sin. Prior to that, it seems our home planet was a place where no man or animal would ever die. Imagine the positive implications inherent in that scenario! Ours would be a world where no human or animal ever took the life of another through violence. War and murder would be unknown. The infirmities of old age would never be suffered by any living creature. The injuries and fatalities resulting from accidents occurring in our present way of life would be non-existent. There would be no sickness and disease, along with their accompanying pain. How very different life on earth would have been had the curse not fallen. What a price we've paid for mankind's decision to disobey God!

But as I said, there is a yet more important truth to be gleaned from the sacrificial death of animals on behalf of Adam and Eve: man cannot make an adequate covering for sin. The garments of fig leaves fashioned by the first man and woman were woefully insufficient. God required something superior. Hebrews 9:22 declares clearly: "... without the *shedding of blood* there is no forgiveness for sin." Forgiveness of sin demands the giving of one life for another, and as the Bible says in Leviticus 17:11: "...the life of a creature is in the blood..." In this case, the life blood spilled was that of innocent animals.

It's important to note that the Lord did not take lightly the death of these sacrificial creatures. All animals have in them "the breath of life," (Genesis 6:17) which originates from God. Thus the life that is given up through the sacrifice of an animal, is ultimately the *life of the Lord Himself.* Being made in the image of God, humans are the highest beings in all the earth, and therefore the most dearly loved by Him. But Scripture reveals that the Lord also cares for the animals.

This truth is particularly established in two parallel passages from the Gospels. In Matthew 10:29 Jesus says: "Are not two sparrows sold for a penny? Yet not one of them falls to the ground apart from the will of your Father." The words "will of" are not in the original Greek text, but were added by the translators. So a more literal rendering would be: "Yet not one of them falls to the ground apart from your Father." Since it is the very life of God which departs from a dying sparrow, He is intimately involved in that loss, and in some sense shares in the consequent grief. In Luke 12:6 Jesus further affirms the Heavenly Father's tenderness toward even the lowliest of His creatures. In spite of the modest market value of sparrows, He points out that: "...not one of them is forgotten by God."

But the death of innocent animals here in Genesis chapter 3, and the later establishment in the Law of God of the requirement of an annual animal sacrifice for the sins of the nation of Israel, foreshadow the ultimate sacrifice which would come thousands of years later. The Creator Himself would arrive in human form as "The Son of God," and literally lay down His own life to redeem us. Through this incredible act of divine love we can find our escape from the second death. This remarkable truth will be explained in more detail in chapter 7 of this book.

A particularly wonderful fact is discovered in the conciliatory garments God made for Adam and Eve. Even in judgment the Lord is merciful. James 2:13 encapsulates a redeeming principal which has been woven into the fabric of every book of the Bible: "Mercy triumphs over judgment!" The terrible curse of sin had brought down the curtain on endless life in the Garden of Eden. It was a dreadful moment. Still, in the twilight of Paradise a symbolic ray of sunshine bursting through a tiny notch in the forbidding mountains at the edge of the horizon promised a day of restoration. God's grace would somehow make a way through the shadows for men and women to again bask in the glow of His blessing. His desire for fellowship with the people He lovingly formed from the dust of the earth would mandate that He provide a means of everlasting reconciliation with them, even while the demands of His righteous justice had now brought punishment for their rebellion.

This divine hope of the ages was deeply needed by

the first humans. God could not allow the sinful couple to live forever on this earth. Their access to the tree of life had to be terminated. The Lord banished them from the Garden of Eden and placed an angel at it's entrance to guard the way back to the tree of life. What happened to Paradise? Why, in so far as we know, has no one ever seen it since Adam and Eve were evicted from it? From the Genesis account we know the general area in which it was located. Why have humans been unable to discover it? Was it obliterated by the cataclysmic flood of Noah's time? Has the Lord simply blinded the eyes of men so that they cannot see the Garden of Eden even when they are there? Did it always exist in, or has it been subsequently moved into another dimension? We have no certain answer, although two passages in the last book of the Bible, Revelation, suggest a likely possibility. But you'll have to wait until chapter 8 of this book for that proposal.

Whatever actually happened to the Garden of Eden, it has been lost for all time to Adam, Eve, and all mankind. And the rest of the earth was dramatically changed from its original state. The newly *cursed* world the man and his wife were about to step into, upon their departure from Paradise, was to be remarkably different from the *blessed* one which had been the only abode they had ever known.

*Not in the original text. Added by the author for clarification.

CHAPTER 3

A Planet Transformed

I doubt Adam and Eve initially grasped the profound impact of their actions. First and foremost, sin had radically changed their relationship with God. God still loved them, but the sacrifice of innocent blood had been required to provide forgiveness for sin and restoration to fellowship. And though they had been forgiven and restored, the man and the woman had been dramatically transformed by the curse of sin. Beyond the physical changes, their souls and spirits were now tainted. The very innocent, intimate bond they had enjoyed with their Maker had now become jaded... to say the least. The relationship that had once flowed so naturally between the Lord and them, had degenerated into one that would now demand constant attention in an often frustrating effort to maintain. We today, even after seeking and receiving God's forgiveness, also experience that same difficulty in sustaining our devotion to Him.

Humans were the *only* beings created in the image of God. From the beginning we had a relationship with Him which is unique among all the other living things. And we were the *only* ones given rulership over the rest of God's creatures. As such, we were God's representatives, or ambassadors, on the earth. We embodied God's ownership of the earth and His authority over it. Satan recognized this, and not only recruited us for his rebellion against the Almighty, but plotted to make us and our planet part of his own kingdom in the process. Through the unbelief and disobedience he produced in Adam and Eve, he achieved his objectives.

In their misguided attempt to become their own gods, the first man and woman had unwittingly turned Satan into the default god of all mankind. Every single one of their descendents would be born estranged from the true God, and would have to be taught how to know, love, and serve Him. This would be a difficult task because the curse of sin had polluted the bodies, souls, and spirits of the father and mother of all human beings, and through them all their progeny. Inadvertently, Adam and Eve had sold us all out to the devil. They had succumbed to the same deception to which all who decide to live their lives by their own rules, ultimately surrender. In attempting to become masters of their own fate, they had become slaves of an evil master named Satan.

The concept that we're all born as sinners comes as a shock, even an offense, to many people. The oft repeated statement "we're *all* God's children," is not entirely true. Original man was God's child, created in His image and likeness (Genesis 1:26, 27), and though that image has been marred by mankind's fall into sin, a semblance of it still remains in us today. We are the offspring of people made by God... *but...* now sold out to the devil! And those of us who do not choose to place the Creator back on His rightful throne in our lives, remain the property of Satan.

Understand, please, that you do not have to be an active member of Anton LaVey's Church of Satan, or some other overtly satanic cult, to be a child of the devil. You simply have to be doing your own thing instead of God's thing. The Lord Jesus Himself once declared to a group of such unrepentant rebels: "You belong to your father, the devil…" (John 8:44). He was not speaking to a satanic cult. He was addressing a religious group who claimed to be worshipping the one true God of Israel! The Apostle John affirmed that it is simply our spiritually fallen ancestry and our sinful personal action, not affiliation with a satanic group, which determine who our father is. "He who does what is sinful is of the devil, because the devil has been sinning from the beginning… This is how we know who the children of God are and who the children of the devil are…" (I John 3:8,10). We are born sinners, and we remain sinners as long as we determine to do our own thing rather than repenting of our sin and surrendering ourselves in faith to the God who made us. We can become the children of God only by being "born again" of the Spirit of the Lord.

It's imperative we recognize that the devil wields his authority over *every individual* born into this world. Like it or not, that includes you and me, my friend, until and unless we are born again. No matter how strong-willed we may think we are, no matter how much we pride ourselves on being "our own person," we are in bondage to a malicious dictator. He may afford us enough slack on the chain to allow us to fool ourselves into thinking we're completely in charge of our lives. But sooner or later we'll feel a jerk on that chain that awakens us to the reality of Satan's control over us.

Speaking of Satan's authority, it extends beyond you and me as individuals. The Lord Jesus Christ Himself cited a "kingdom" belonging to the devil (Matthew 12:26, Mark 3:23,24, Luke 11:18), and twice it's recorded that He referred to the devil as "the prince of this *world*." (John 12:31, John 14:30). The Apostle Paul (II Corinthians 4:4) called Satan "The god of this *age*..." and the Apostle John (I John 5:19) declared "...the whole *world* is under the control of the evil one." While in the original texts the Greek word for "world" primarily means the earth, and the Greek word for "age" chiefly refers to a particular time period, both words are frequently used to denote "the world system." We can safely understand these Scriptures to be telling us that as a consequence of the fall of man, the devil became, and continues to be, ruler of this current world system. He did so by overcoming, and then displacing, the earthly governors originally appointed by the Lord: Adam and Eve.

Curiously, in some manner, Satan's kingdom is headquartered in the atmosphere. Ephesians 2:2 describes the devil as "..the ruler of the kingdom of the air...", and in Ephesians 6:12 his subordinates are described as "... spiritual forces of evil in the heavenly realms."

The earth may still belong to God, but the world system under which the fallen human race operates on earth is part of the devil's kingdom. And the Bible tells us that Satan is assisted in the administration of this kingdom by a myriad of evil underlings, variously referred to as demons, evil (or unclean) spirits, rulers, authorities, powers of this dark world, and spiritual forces of evil.

In response to an accusation that He Himself drove out demons by the power of Beelzebub (one of the previously mentioned names of Satan), Jesus made it plain that this accusation against Him was false. Christ confirmed however; that demons were part of Satan's kingdom, operating under the devil's authority (Matthew 12:25-28). And human beings, who were meant to be the expression of the Lord's authority, have become (except for those who have been born again) the pawns of the devil. What a revolting development! The Apostle John explains that this Satanically controlled world system is the wellspring of all evil human behavior. "For everything in the world -- the cravings of sinful man, the lust of his eyes and the boasting of what he has and does -- comes not from the Father, but from the world." (I John 2:16)

Having established that the prevailing world system and every individual in it has, through original sin, come under the control of such a malevolent regime, we can no longer be surprised that there is so much evil and suffering in this life. Indeed, were it not for the grace and mercy of God, we would expect that a planet under Satan's influence would be an even worse environment than it is. Everything God created initially had a good and beneficial purpose. But under the curse of sin and the influence of the devil, those good purposes have been diminished and even distorted.

Yet another terrible transformation had taken place as an effect of the curse. I touched on it briefly in chapter 2, but now I want to deal with it more extensively. Some specifics of this overall effect were spelled out in the sentences that fell upon the snake, the devil, the woman, and the man in Genesis chapter 3. But the broader implications are later captured by the passage in Romans 8:20,21, which was quoted in part in the previous chapter. "For the creation was subjected to frustration, not by its own choice, but by the will of the one who subjected it, in hope that the creation itself will be liberated from its bondage to decay and brought into the glorious freedom of the children of God." As noted in that earlier chapter of this book, *decay* speaks of death. The Greek word translated "decay" in this passage literally means "perishableness." It signifies a process of becoming increasingly inferior in quality, to the point where ultimately life ceases. And the whole "creation" was brought into bondage to this process. Creation, of course, includes our entire planet, and decay is evident everywhere on earth.

Scientists have observed this pattern, and codified it in the second law of thermodynamics. Also known as the law of entropy, this principle essentially states that left to themselves, all systems go from organized (or complex) to disorganized (or random). Incidentally, this law, which has been repeatedly tested by experiments and is universally accepted as fact by the scientific community, flies in the face of the theory of evolution. The premise of evolutionary theory is that complex life forms evolved on their own through chance and time from simple life forms... which had themselves evolved from inanimate material. This *premise* of evolution is an impossibility given the *fact* of the law of entropy.

The effects of the second law of thermodynamics, described in Scripture as "bondage to decay," can be observed throughout the universe. Some examples can only be detected by trained scientists with advanced instruments. The sun, for example, is slowly burning out.

Our moon is gradually moving away from the earth. The strength of earth's electromagnetic field is decreasing exponentially. All of these instances of decay have had, or if given more time will have, a negative effect upon life on earth. Many other examples, such as the life and death cycles of plants and animals, can be easily seen around us in our everyday lives. Even inorganic things, such as our man-made machines, in many ways demonstrate the outcome of decay. Everyone who has ever bought a shiny new car knows that it will someday wear out and end up as scrap in the junkyard.

Perhaps no where is decay more evident to us than in our own bodies, especially as we grow older. Through this process all people are moving inexorably toward that dreaded rendezvous with death. Even if we die in an accident or from an act of violence, it's still the result of some aspect of the curse. However; in most cases, death does not come about suddenly, but gradually, through the body's slow breakdown from aging or disease. This is the most personal demonstration of the effects of decay.

From Adam and Eve onward, all mankind became subject to the decay that leads to death. But the progress toward the body's eventual failure was much slower for the earliest generations. Indeed, the average lifespan of the individuals listed in Genesis chapter 5, excluding Enoch (who was uniquely taken to be with the Lord under special circumstances at age 365), was 908 years! The relinquishing of our bodies to decay accelerated rapidly after the flood of Noah's time (I'll discuss that in greater depth in chapter 5), until today, our average life span has been reduced to roughly 70 to 80 years. This is virtually unchanged in the approximately 3,000 years since the

Scriptures declared in Psalm 90:10: "The length of our days is seventy years -- or eighty, if we have the strength..."

My mother once told me that there comes a point in life beyond which we don't get any older on the *inside*. We observe the elderly person staring back at us from the mirror and incredulously declare: "That's not me!" Growing old is not exactly fun. We discover that our energy and strength diminish with the passing of years, while our aches and pains increase. We're troubled by minds and memories which slowly lose acumen. Mirrors and photos alert us to unwelcome changes in our appearance. Grey hairs, receding hairlines, wrinkles, and generally rearranged bodies confront us with the depressing reality that we're aging. While it is true that there are some advantages to growing older... we can't seem to remember what they are! Even if we could recall those compensations, given the choice, most of us would unhesitatingly select the advantages of youth over those of aging. But alas, we have no choice. We are "in bondage to decay."

As pointed out, disease also greatly contributes to this process of the decay of our bodies. Sickness was not part of God's original plan for creation, but was another result of the curse. Human disease has many causes, all of which came into existence after the fall of man in the Garden of Eden. Some of these causes are intrinsic. For instance, it's widely believed in the medical community that all of us have cancer cells in our bodies. Whether these cells develop into the full-blown disease depends on certain conditions. Other illnesses are inherent in the body through genetic transmission from our parents. A few common examples of these are type 1 diabetes, cystic fibrosis, and polycystic kidney disease.

An important point to be made about these disorders is that they are the result of genetic mutation in previous generations. Science has proven that the overwhelming majority of genetic mutations are *detrimental* at best, and *lethal* at worst. This is significant because it coincides with the aforementioned second law of thermodynamics, and presents an insurmountable obstacle to the theory of evolution, which depends upon innumerable *beneficial* genetic mutations over many generations, for the development of higher life forms.

Another deleterious effect of the curse on our genes is demonstrated in deformities which frequently occur in the offspring of close relatives who marry. Such marriages are commonly considered incestuous, and in much of the world are forbidden by law. And in fact, these kind of relationships were strictly forbidden by the Law of God in the 18th chapter of Leviticus. However; that Law was not instituted until a few thousand years after the time of Adam and Eve. Indeed, their sons would have had to marry their sisters in order to propagate the human race.

The genetic degeneration which often produces abnormalities in the children of parents who are close biological family members, is the effect of the accumulation of generations of genetic mistakes initiated by the curse. Adam and Eve were created *perfect...* with *perfect* genes. As we've already indicated, genetic degeneration is a consequence of the curse. And it was only after many generations of genetic mutations had accumulated, that such inter-marriage became a problem and was forbidden by the Lord. I should add here, that genetic damage likely has been multiplied by the effects of the increased ultraviolet rays (as will be explained in chapter 5) humans have been exposed to in the aftermath of the worldwide flood.

Other illnesses have their origins in microscopic life forms such as bacteria and viruses. As with all life forms on the planet, bacteria and viruses were created by God to be totally positive, and in harmony with all other life, but were corrupted in various measures by the curse. Some of these microorganisms still are beneficial to us. The harmful ones enter our bodies in diverse ways. They invade through the air, food and drink, injury, and intimate contact with other people. Once they arrive they are battled by our bodies' own immune systems, immune systems which unfortunately have been compromised by the curse. As amazing as our bodies still are, they no longer maintain the unmatched abilities and perfection of the original bodies of Adam and Eve. Even when enhanced by healthy lifestyles and supplemented by the best the various medical sciences have to offer, our immunity still suffers from the limitations imposed by the curse.

Besides the inherited components of human illness derived from Adam and Eve's original sin, present societal and individual sin can also have a direct detrimental impact upon our health. Many diseases are promoted by the perverted lifestyles and cultures of fallen humanity. Just as our individual personalities are the outcome of not just genetics alone, but environment and personal choice as well, so is disease. Unresolved anger, bitterness, hatred, jealousy, worry, sexual promiscuity, unhealthy diet, inadequate exercise, environmental pollution, and other factors have advanced sickness in our world. These issues, which are essentially the result of the moral decay of human culture, plus the added component of individual sin, are among the multiple products of the curse.

In spite of tremendous advances in both conventional and natural medicine, the human race continues to be plagued by disease. Though some illnesses seem to have been eradicated, even these occasionally poke through the fabric of medical science to remind us of our mortality. Sometimes these old bacterial and viral foes develop innovative tactics to overcome our defenses. New sicknesses continue to arise to engage us in battle. Even with our unrelenting efforts to fight them, the number of cases of certain diseases (heart disease, cancer, and diabetes, for example) increase just as relentlessly as our medical progress. We may be able to prevent some diseases and cure others, but sickness will always be a major aspect of life in this sin-cursed world. Someday, those of us who have committed our lives to Jesus Christ will receive a new and perfect body, not subject to sickness or death. "Meanwhile we groan, longing to be clothed with our heavenly dwelling..." (II Corinthians 5:2).

Decay and death are also frequently hastened by the violence of man against man. This, too, is a result of the fall and the curse of sin. The first murder in history is recorded in Genesis chapter 4. It involved two of Adam and Eve's sons: Cain and Abel. It further demonstrates the effect of the curse on all human beings. The predisposition to sin has been passed on genetically to all the descendents of the first man and woman. And while Eve had to be tempted by the serpent... and Adam by Eve... no outside entity is now required to lead us into sin. The "sin gene" is inherent in our nature.

No one has to teach us how to sin. We are born

sinners. King David lamented in Psalm 51:5: "Surely I was sinful at birth, sinful from the time my mother conceived me." In Romans 7:20 the Apostle Paul describes this condition as "...sin living in me." James 1:14 informs us that as a consequence of this condition, temptation can rise from *within* us: "...but each one is tempted when, by his own evil desire, he is dragged away and enticed." That's not to say the devil no longer lures people into sin, it simply means that temptation can arise *internally* without his direct intervention. Recognizing this principle makes it easy to understand why violence has unfortunately become such an integral part of the human experience.

Thus, Cain needed no snake possessed by Satan to suggest he murder his brother, Abel. The sin principle lived within him, waiting to enter his heart and find expression through his actions. That's why the Lord forewarned Cain: "...sin is crouching at your door..." (Genesis 4:7) The story in Genesis of the first homicide relates how, in reaction to the Lord's acceptance of his brother's sacrifice and rejection of his own sacrifice, Cain became angry with God and jealous of his brother. The scriptural account in Genesis 4 does not specify exactly why Cain's sacrifice was rejected and Abel's accepted, although Hebrews 11:4 later informs us that faith (or the lack thereof) played a major role in the different view the Almighty took of their sacrifices.

I'll not take the time here to suggest a number of possibilities postulated by Bible scholars as to the cause of God's acceptance of one brother's sacrifice and rejection of the other's. Suffice it to say that the context implies Cain knew he had not done right in the offering of his sacrifice to the Lord. But instead of repenting and making it right, he fostered his anger. God, who always knows the minds and hearts of men, recognized that left to run its course, his bitterness would produce sinful actions. So He lovingly counseled him, advising him where his attitude would lead. Cain, however, did not heed the Lord's advice.

Anger led to bitterness, bitterness cultivated hatred, and hatred gave birth to murder. How long this progression took we're not told. But in due course Cain said to Abel: "Let's go out into the field." (Genesis 4:8) Whether an angry exchange led to a crime of passion or a cold-blooded, premeditated scheme was played out, the encounter ended with Cain attacking and killing his own brother. This first recorded murder is also our opening lesson in the school of inequities. It teaches us the fact that on our distressingly transformed planet, the good do sometimes die young. It was a tragic episode. But it was only the first drop in a torrent of violent death which, in its reckless rush through the valley of human history, has come to far exceed the ferocity of the famed raging Colorado River. And the genuine headwaters of this raging river of immorality and violence are to be found in the "post-sin" Garden of Eden. True, not all human beings have become killers, but the potential abides in all. And too many have fulfilled that potential. This brutal path to death and decay also stems from the curse.

Of course, the murder of one individual by another was just the start. Mass murderers kill many others, some taking the life of one victim at a time, others killing many people at the same time in the same place. Then there are madmen who become dictators and slaughter hundreds, thousands, or even millions.

Finally, war is probably the most prolific killer of humans

by deliberate violent means. The Apostle James attributes all these fatal human conflicts to the same genetically inherited selfish motives of covetousness, jealousy, and anger that led Cain to slay his brother, Abel. "What causes fights and quarrels among you? Don't they come from your desires that battle within you? You want something but you don't get it. You kill and covet, but you cannot have what you want. You quarrel and fight." (James 4:1,2) These are also the fruits of the world system cited previously in this chapter, through our quotation of I John 2:16. The sinful, fallen nature, encouraged by the devil inspired world system, led Cain to murder his brother. It is that same disposition which, if nurtured enough, produces the Joseph Stalins, Adolph Hitlers, Idi Amins, Saddam Husseins, and Osama Bin Ladens of the world. War, terrorism, and other forms of genocide all have their roots in the curse. But this was not the way God intended life on earth to be.

In the beginning, *all* creation, not just humankind, had lived in full harmony. All life forms on earth not only did no harm to others, they actually contributed to the well being of others in some capacity. And each had its unique place in God's design and order. As God's special representatives, Adam and Eve were at the top of this order of created beings. Together they enjoyed the approval of the Lord and brought Him glory.

But that all changed as the curse opened the door for the development of this hostile, competitive, carnivorous environment in which we now live. Still, traces of the original harmony of creation remain, and can be occasionally seen in the lofty heights of selfless nobility to which humans can rise in caring for one another. It can even be glimpsed in the way some animals still contribute to the welfare of others. But the images of these beautiful associations are marred by the specter of the ugly animosity that characterizes the prominent darker side of nature. And not only do humans and many animals kill and devour one another, plants also interact similarly with other life forms.

Let me interject here that it's unclear whether on God's original earth individual plants died. Plants are a very different kind of life than man and animals. All animals possess the breath of life. That breath or "spirit" is an impartation from God which plants do not have. It's evident that humans and their fellow fauna were not meant to die. It's not so obvious whether that immortality applied to plants, too. Yet, I suspect that in keeping with the general nature of things back then, plants did not die either.

However uncertain that issue may be, we do know that today various kinds of vegetation die not only from being eaten by animals, killed by man-made chemicals, and destroyed by natural diseases and disasters, but also die by the process of decay that now plagues all life. Plants even destroy each other in competition for the soil. And while plants generally still provide nutrition for people and animals as God intended in the beginning, I believe the level of nutrition they offer is not as great as it once was. And some plants actually bring harm to us with things like thorns and poisons. A few plants (the Venus flytrap, for example) actually eat animals. Like animals, plants have been profoundly affected by the curse of sin.

This transformation of the character of relationships among living things... from mutually beneficial, to competitive and even antagonistic... also extends to the microscopic level. We know that while there are beneficial bacteria which are vital to life, many others bring sickness and death to animals and humans. There are even numerous bacteria and viruses that relentlessly consume *one another.* It's not perfectly clear whether all of these various changes took place immediately after the original sin, or were instituted through gradual change. But we can say that they all occurred *after* the curse fell.

Some historical evidences actually confront us with the possibility that the intellectual ability of human beings has suffered decay… that our ancestors were superior to us in that capacity. This would be inconsistent with the evolutionary view of man which depicts early humans as more brutish and less intelligent than their modern descendents. But it would certainly be consistent with the previously mentioned definition of the Greek word for decay found in Romans 8:21. I pointed out that it "signifies a process of becoming increasingly inferior in quality."

There are accounts stating the great Persian conqueror Cyrus knew the name of every man in his army. Even conservative numbers place the size of that army in the tens of thousands. If that report of Cyrus is true, it would indicate his memory abilities were beyond that of even modern day geniuses, reaching perhaps into the quirky realm of savant-like mental skills. And it would not be the only such ancient testimony. It was said that Lucius Scipio knew the names of all the Roman people, and Mithridates of Pontus could speak all 22 languages of the peoples in his domain.

Author and lecturer Ian Taylor, addresses this fascinating topic. He suggests that if the commonly held assertion is true, that the average person uses only 10 percent of their brain's capacity, and only geniuses use substantially more, it raises an interesting question about the theory of evolution. He inquires how it's possible evolutionary mechanisms provided us with brain capability so much exceeding our use of it? That would be inconsistent with the mindless methods of natural selection. How could such an accidental process anticipate the future mental requirements of humans? Taylor asserts: "...the genius... can then be better explained on the basis of unusual retention of ancestral brain capacity rather than prolepsis *(a provision in anticipation of something not yet known to be needed)* of an evolutionary aspiration." He proposes that this issue obliges us to consider the possibility that ancient man used his full brain capacity, and that modern man (with the possible exception of geniuses) no longer can or does.

Even some evolutionists believe that our ancestors possessed more intelligence than we moderns do. Nobel prize winner Robert Klark Graham, asserted that ancient humans were intellectually superior to their contemporary counterparts. Citing the larger brain size and impressive accomplishments of so-called Cro-Magnon men, he states: "Humankind never again reached such a state of average excellence. Apparently this peak was reached only by the early Cro-Magnons. Later generations of these same peoples were not quite the equal of their forebears. Their workmanship was less admirable. This was the first known regression in the development of our kind." Graham was so deeply concerned over this intellectual decline that in 1979 he co-founded a sperm bank, consisting of donations from geniuses, in hopes of halting this deterioration by replenishing the population with highly intelligent children through artificial insemination.

Indeed, the achievements of various ancient peoples (Egyptians, Sumerians, Mayans, etc.) leave many grasping for explanations as curious as that of proposing that such accomplishments were actually achieved as the result of extra-terrestrial visitations. Though their theories of the cause of this possible decline in brain power may differ from our suggestion that it could be the effect of the "decay" resulting from the Edenic curse, their recognition of this apparent intellectual regression lends credence to our basic hypothesis. Another book could easily be filled with more data corroborating this supposition. Instead, please allow me to briefly highlight just a handful more specifics.

Various ancient artifacts offer support of ancient man's sophistication. At the turn of the 20th century an object was recovered from a ship which had sunk in the Aegean Sea more than 2,000 years ago. Known as the "Antikythera Mechanism," this object has been thoroughly studied by modern scientists. It was determined to be constructed of numerous sophisticated gears, so sophisticated in fact, that some found it hard to accept that it could be so *old*. Models of this mechanism were built, and it was ascertained to be a rather complex analog computer... an automated calculator probably used for astronomical and navigational purposes.

Geologist, archeologist, and creation science researcher, Dr. Dennis Swift, owns a substantial collection of very old artifacts. He's amassed these during his many trips around the world, during which he conducts research in conjunction with local scientific institutions.

One of the artifacts in his possession which has particularly fascinated me is an obsidian (a type of volcanic glass) scalpel found in the tomb of a Peruvian surgeon, dated at 600-700 A.D. Ancient Peruvian surgeons have been found to have performed advanced operations once thought to be practiced only by modern doctors, including complex brain surgeries! Their medical tools reflect that kind of sophistication. Obsidian scalpels, such as the one possessed by Dr. Swift, can be sharpened to incredible levels. Observed under powerful magnification, their edges still appear keen, while those of modern surgical steel scalpels look uneven and irregular. The obsidian blade's cutting edge is so precise that its use does not bruise the skin, resulting in more rapid healing and diminished scarring.

Dr. Donald Chittick served for many years as chairman of the Department of Natural Sciences at George Fox University in Oregon. He's also a professor of chemistry, an inventor, and a lecturer and author. He devotes much of his book "The Puzzle of Ancient Man" to consideration of numerous evidences of superior intelligence in our ancestors, found at scenes of early human activity.

He cites the markings on the surface of the Nazca Desert in Peru, a location made famous in the 1970's by Erich Von Daniken's book: "Chariots of the Gods?" These gigantic precisely straight lines and accomplished artistic images are remarkable even by today's standards. Yet they're estimated to be at least 1,000 years old, and perhaps as much as 4,000 years old. Intriguingly, they're only clearly visible from above, as viewed by modern aircraft. There are even credible archeological indications that the Nazca people may have created and used flying machines!

And these are not the only evidences of ancient flight.

Strikingly modern-like designs, accounts and descriptions of prehistoric aircraft are found in divergent parts of the world, including what appears to be a delta-winged jet aircraft model discovered in Columbia, and conventional looking model monoplanes found in an Egyptian tomb.

Dr. Chittick also calls our attention to the ruins of the city of Sacsahuaman in Peru. The precision and size of the stones used in its construction are amazing. One stone in particular is calculated to weigh 20,000 tons. It's doubtful that we have the technology today to move this huge block, yet the builders of Sacsahuaman did so a projected 600 years ago! One of the most compelling cases Dr. Chittick mentions is that of the Mayan calendar. More than 2,000 years ago they had calculated the length of a year to be 365.2420 days. With the use of modern scientific instruments, we've now determined that the exact length of a year is 365.2422 days. Without the use of our contemporary devices, and our advanced expertise (built upon centuries of accumulated astronomical studies), the Mayans of antiquity were within two-ten-thousandths of a day of that precise figure!

This information is but the proverbial tip of the iceberg. Archaeologist Jonathan Gray, in his book "Dead Men's Secrets," has catalogued many hundreds of authenticated historical discoveries, compiling a powerful case for the existence of superior human intelligence millennia ago. The vast evidences of higher scientific and technical abilities among ancient people suggest that the decay, caused by the curse pronounced in the Garden of Eden, may have indeed diminished the capabilities of the human mind. And this very real possibility runs counter to the theory of evolution, which insists that life forms become higher, more complex, and more sophisticated through chance mutations and the passage of time. It would appear that the Bible's account of the origin and development of life on earth far better explains current conditions than Darwin's notion of naturalistic selection. In the real world we observe more *regression* than *progression*.

Having considered some of the major revolutionary changes to our world brought about by the disobedience and rebellion of Adam and Eve, we might ask if there is any aspect of life on this planet which has not been plagued by the curse? It hardly seems so. Its scope and effect have been truly pervasive! The resulting perversions, inconsistencies, and problems are unnatural to the world of order and harmony which God originally created. These changes were all ushered in by the Edenic curse. Yet the downward slide was not complete with the features of this curse listed in Genesis chapter 3. More trouble was brewing. And a catastrophic event on the distant horizon was waiting to generate still further negative transformations.

CHAPTER 4

The Worldwide Flood

I t's one of the most well-known stories of the Bible. Millions of children hear of Noah and the ark in Sunday school, long before they enter the secondary educational system to begin their formal study of history. But the account of this worldwide flood has been under relentless attack by skeptics for the last two centuries. They've narrowed the scope of the worldwide deluge to that of a limited local flood, they've re-interpreted it as a symbolic story rather than a literal account, and it's even been dismissed as total mythology by some critics. Regardless, no event, outside of the original curse in Genesis chapter 3, has so transformed the planet as the worldwide flood. And despite the naysayers, no other ancient narrative is buttressed by the records of so many disparate cultures and so much physical evidence. This chapter and the following one will relate much of this supporting data for your consideration.

The flood of Noah's day was another sin-triggered curse. In a sense it was an extension of the curse initiated by the original fall of man in Paradise. Earlier, I introduced you to that part of the Edenic curse which affected the ground. (Genesis 3:17) The flood was a *further* curse upon the ground, resulting from the bad behavior of mankind, just as the first curse had. After the deluge God promised: "Never again will I curse the ground because of man…" (Genesis 8:21).

The same Hebrew word is used for "ground" in both passages, and notably it comes from the identical root word as the name, "Adam." It primarily means "soil." In other places in Scripture it's also rendered: "country," "earth," "ground," and "land." From the context it's obvious that in Genesis 3:17 the word is best understood as "soil," while in the aftermath of the flood in Genesis 8:21 it's likely best interpreted as "land." But the bottom line is clear, the deluge was a *curse* upon the earth. Thankfully, as you'll later learn, the Lord in His love and mercy would manage to bring good out of this calamity. A prophecy of this is presented in Genesis 5:28,29: "When Lamech had lived 182 years, he had a son. He named him Noah [meaning rest or comfort]* and said, 'He will comfort us in the labor and painful toil of our hands caused by the ground the LORD has cursed."

The Scriptural account of the deluge begins in Genesis chapter 6. "When men began to increase in number on the earth and daughters were born to them, the sons of God saw that the daughters of men were beautiful, and they married any of them they chose. Then the LORD said, 'My Spirit will not contend with man forever, for he is mortal; his days will be a hundred and twenty years.' The Nephilim were on the earth in those days - and also afterward - when the sons of God went to the daughters of men and had children by them. They were the heroes of old, men of renown. The LORD saw how great man's wickedness on the earth had become, and that every inclination of the thoughts of his heart was only evil all the time. The LORD was grieved that he had made man on the earth, and his heart was filled with pain. So the LORD said, 'I will wipe mankind, whom I have created, from the face of the earth - men and animals, and creatures that move along the ground, and birds of the air - for I am grieved that I have made them.' But Noah found favor in the eyes of the LORD." (Genesis 6:1-8).

In the estimated 16 or 17 centuries from the expulsion of mankind out of Paradise, to the time described in this passage, human society had degenerated to an incredible low. Any group of people which rebels against God's benevolent reign and rejects His absolute moral standards in favor of fallen humanity's satanically corrupted morals, will ultimately descend into an abyss of malevolence. The most telling part of the description of this era is found in the Lord's observation of man in Genesis 6:5 that: "... every inclination of the thoughts of his heart was only *evil all the time.*" How pervasive this appalling condition was, is emphasized by the fact that in this verse the Word of God refers to all humanity in the *singular.* It speaks of *man's* wickedness, not *men's* wickedness. And it refers to *his heart,* not *their hearts.* With the exception of Noah and his family, the *whole* human race had become incredibly wicked.

Especially because we live in an era dominated by access to mass media, you and I have witnessed a remarkable amount of evil. Still, nothing in our time appears to approach the scale of immorality described here. What could possibly explain this remarkable slide into the depths of depravity? Sin is, of course, at the root of it. All these people were born sinners. And simply stated, sinners sin! What else would you expect? Further, sin is addictive. One sin leads to more sin.

As often happens with any addiction, repeated consumption at the entry level, eventually becomes bland. So then sin must be taken to another level to achieve the temporary pleasure we crave. This cycle then repeats itself. Unrestrained, it becomes a never ending downward spiral. If we haven't personally known someone who's taken this ride to the depths of wantonness, we've all at least heard or read of such a person. But we've never yet lived in a civilization *fully dominated* by these kind of people. It appears something even more powerful than the genetically inherited sin nature must have been at work in society by the time of Noah.

I believe verses 2 and 4 of Genesis chapter 6 hold the key to unlocking this mystery. Genesis 6:2 informs us that the "sons of God" were drawn to the beauty of the "daughters of men," and married any of them they pleased. Genesis 6:4 further implies that the offspring of these mixed marriages were the "Nephilim." This is one of the more enigmatic, and therefore controversial passages in the Bible. The controversy centers primarily around the identification of the "sons of God" cited in Genesis 6:2. Determining that identification with *total* confidence is hardly possible. But weighing the evidence carefully will bring us to the most likely conclusion. I won't take the space here to deal with the matter as thoroughly as I might like. However; I will give you what I feel are the bare essentials of the issue, and declare to you what I believe is the best explanation.

Let's begin with the main issue of who the "sons of

God" actually were. Many Bible scholars contend that they were the godly male descendents of Seth, who was introduced in Genesis 5:3 as a son of Adam and Eve. The "daughters of men" are then identified as the ungodly female descendents of Cain. This interpretation characterizes the mingling of these two groups as an early example of the disastrous results of mixed marriages between believers and unbelievers.

But I see problems with this hypothesis. First and foremost, there is no indication either in this passage, or anywhere else in the Scripture, that these "sons of God" were the descendents of Seth, or that these "daughters of men" were the descendents of Cain! Secondly, this interpretation would hardly explain the unprecedented prevalence of extreme wickedness in the population of that day. I have seen mixed marriages of believers and unbelievers result in several outcomes. In some fortunate cases the unbelieving spouse eventually becomes a believer. In many cases the believing spouse backslides. If the unbelieving spouse remains unconverted and the believing spouse maintains their faith, they either spend a lifetime with some measure of regret at being unequally yoked, or the unhappy union ends in the tragedy of divorce. I have witnessed all of these outcomes from a mixed marriage. But I have never seen any hint that spiritually mixed marriages would lead to the mass transformation of society into a cesspool of sin.

In my view, the more biblical and reasonable identification of the "sons of God" in Genesis 6:2, is that they were fallen angels. This position is supported by the witness of the ancient Jewish Fathers and the early Christian Fathers. The Hebrew phrase here translated "sons of God" is used throughout the Old Testament to refer not to *human* beings, but to *angelic* beings. If we understand the expression "sons of God" in this context to be speaking of *fallen* angels, then the whole story begins to make sense. This interpretation also lines up with a couple of related New Testament passages.

You may recall that in a brief description of who the devil was, in chapter one of this book, I told you that he led a rebellion against God. After his defeat, he and his minions, consisting of one-third of the angels in heaven, were cast down to earth. These are subsequently described as "fallen angels." I'm convinced they're the ones who intermarried with the "daughters of men," that is, women who were simply human. The intermingling of human sin genes with that of unredeemable fallen angels would explain what appears to be a colossal increase in iniquity by the time of Noah. The offspring of these accursed marriages are appropriately called "the Nephilim" in Genesis 6:4. Nephilim comes from a Hebrew root word meaning "fallen one!"

This view is reinforced by II Peter 2:4: "...God did not spare angels when they sinned, but sent them to hell, putting them into gloomy dungeons to be held for judgment..." Jude 6 says much the same: "And angels who did not keep their positions of authority, but abandoned their own home -- these He has kept in darkness, bound with everlasting chains for judgment on the great Day." The Bible teaches that there are fallen angels, also known as demons and evil (or unclean) spirits, who work with Satan *here on earth*. So why are *these particular* fallen angels mentioned in II Peter and Jude presently confined to dungeons in *hell*? Besides their participation with the rest of the seditious angels in the devil's rebellion against God, what terrible additional sin did they commit that led to this dark, gloomy imprisonment?

With both of these passages, a clue is given in the very next verse. Peter related the deeds of these fallen angels to the ungodly people at the time of the flood, and the wicked populations of the cities of Sodom and Gomorrah. (II Peter 2:5,6) Jude also compared the deeds and consequences of the fallen angels with the sexual perversion and resulting punishment of the inhabitants of Sodom and Gomorrah. (Jude 7) It should be noted that in the final hours before judgment fell, male inhabitants of Sodom tried to have perverse sexual relations with the *angels* who came to rescue the righteous man, Lot, and His family. This makes it rather easy to connect *fallen angels* with the "sons of God" in Genesis chapter 6.

An otherwise puzzling passage in I Corinthians 11:10, may shed even more light on this scenario. In referring to the edict for a woman to cover her head in deference to the first woman being made *from* man, and *for* man, which edict was mentioned earlier in in verses 5-9 of chapter 11, verse 10 adds: "For this reason, and because of the *angels*, the woman ought to have a sign of authority on her head." Could it be that the Apostle Paul was concerned that the alluring beauty of a woman's hair could again tempt fallen angels?

One might argue against the possibility of angelic beings marrying humans based upon the indication Jesus gave in Matthew 22:30 that angels do not marry. But a closer look at this text demonstrates that when proclaiming this unmarried status, the Lord was specifically speaking of "the angels *in heaven.*" The angels referred to as the sons of God in Genesis 6:2 had been *cast out of heaven.*

The intermarrying of women with fallen angels would certainly better explain the extreme wickedness on the planet at the time of Noah, than would the intermarrying of the male descendents of Seth with the female descendents of Cain. This interpretation also better explains the name and characteristics of their progeny, the Nephilim. As half breed children of fallen angels they probably inherited some of the great size and strength of angels. This could be why Genesis 6:4 describes them as "...heroes of old, men of renown." Lest the term "heroes" mislead you into thinking these must have been *good men*, let me clarify. The original Hebrew word translated "hero" in this text simply means: "mighty one or mighty warrior." It does not automatically carry with it the connotation of *good* character or deeds. In fact, this same Hebrew word is found in Isaiah 5:22, which proclaims: "woe to those who are *heroes* at drinking wine and champions at mixing drinks..."

With the aid of the divinely prohibited union between mankind and fallen angels, sin and it's rot had accelerated. The planet had been driven into a desperate condition. "Now the earth was corrupt in God's sight and was full of violence. God saw how corrupt the earth had become, for all the people on earth had corrupted their ways." (Genesis 6:11,12) All of this grieved the Lord and filled his heart with pain.

What was it about the state of mankind that filled God's heart with pain? There were many facts contributing to His anguish. They had plummeted far from the lofty purposes for which they had been created as God's representatives.

They had rebelled against the Lord's commands and principles, and turned to lives of sin. Instead of a peaceful environment, the world had developed into a vicious cauldron of violence.

But more than anything else, it was His loss of intimacy with people that broke God's heart. The inhabitants of earth had turned away from the precious fellowship with God for which He had created them. Instead, they had given themselves over to Satan… the very entity who had stolen Paradise from mankind in the first place. Through interbreeding with the devil's allies they may have inherited some of the physical strength and mental power which allowed them to become "heroes" and "men of renown" in the estimation of their peers, but God regarded them as "corrupt!" In fact, they were so corrupt that the only way to purge the earth of such evil was to *wipe them all out.*

A further curse for sin was about to fall. The Lord had determined that only drastic action could turn things around. He declared destruction for all the people and the whole planet. But, thank God, in the midst of this ungodly society was *one man* who walked with God… *one man* who had not polluted himself with the incredible evil which had conquered the rest of humanity. This *one man* prevented the total extinction of *mankind*!

Had it not been for the righteousness of Noah, the entire human race would have been destroyed in the flood. Only God knows where the course of events would have turned from there. Maybe the Lord would have started over with a new first man and woman. He might have produced a completely novel and different race of creatures. Or He could have decided that the possibility of any beings on the planet prevailing over the control of sin and Satan was hopeless, and the flood would be the absolute end of any such race!

"But Noah found favor in the eyes of the Lord." The Hebrew word in the original text of Genesis 6:8 quoted above is not fully represented by the English word "favor." The root word properly means "to bend or stoop in kindness *to an inferior.*" It's used to imply not simply favor, but the showing of *mercy, pity, and grace.* Noah was a righteous man, but neither he, nor any human being before or since (except Jesus Christ) could achieve the perfection that would allow God to bestow favor, goodness, or kindness that is *fully deserved.* The concept of *undeserved* divine favor, commonly referred to as the "grace of God," is essential to understanding the Creator's relationship with individuals, and humanity as a whole. Noah's heart attitude of righteousness drew God to him and his family, but only "grace" allowed the Lord to spare their lives.

God was about to do what He would have to do repeatedly throughout human history. Each time mankind turned irretrievably away from their Maker, in His compassion the Lord would start over with a man who truly loved Him. God would begin anew with a person who longed for the kind of intimate fellowship with Him that He had intended from the beginning to be the essence of His relationship with human beings. He found such an individual in Noah.

So while God planned to destroy the earth with a flood, he commanded Noah to prepare an ark which would be the means of sparing his family (his wife, sons: Shem, Ham, and Japheth, and their wives) and a representative group of the animals. While those of us who have heard the story of the deluge know that this ark served as a boat of sorts, the Hebrew word here literally means a *box*. It's used in only two passages in the Old Testament: here, and in the story in Exodus chapter 2 of the floating basket Moses' mother made to save her son's life. The ark probably resembled a barge more than a boat.

Noah's ark was a very large vessel constructed of cypress wood and covered with pitch. It measured approximately 450 feet long (one and a half times the length of a football field), 75 feet wide, and 45 feet high. Through laboratory testing of scale models, it's been determined that these dimensions made the ark a uniquely stable vessel for use on the high seas. It would have been extremely difficult to capsize. And it would have had the cargo capacity of roughly 520 railroad box cars! Given the scientifically proven potential for diversification of animals through breeding, this would have been more than enough room for a pair of all of the types of creatures necessary for the continuation of each species, as well as the later development of their various intra-species breeds, after the flood.

The ark was built with 3 decks (each having numerous rooms), a roof, a side door, and a window. Noah was told that 2 (one male, one female) of every kind of creature would come to him, and that he was to store enough food on the ark to feed them all. (Genesis 6:19-21) Additionally, the Lord specified that he was to take 7 of every kind of clean animal, and 2 of every kind of *unclean* animal with him. (Genesis 7:2) This order was given to Noah long before the laws God later gave Moses defined the differences between clean and unclean animals, but we may assume that these distinctions were much the same as in the later Law, and were understood by Noah. This provision for more clean than unclean animals to survive the flood, was probably because clean animals (such as cattle and sheep) were more useful to humans, and approved for sacrifice to God.

For an undetermined period of years, Noah, his sons, and perhaps some hired laborers, worked to complete the ark. This length of time was probably at least several decades, and perhaps as long as the 120 years mentioned in Genesis 6:3. That 120 years seems to be a season of grace occurring between the Lord's decision to destroy the earth and the actual start of the flood.

Besides building the ark, the Genesis account does not specify what else Noah may have been doing during this time. However; we do have some strong hints elsewhere in the Bible. First, God's pattern throughout Scripture has always been to use His chosen people as witnesses for Him to those around them, seeking through their witness to bring others to faith in Himself. Secondly, the Apostle Peter calls Noah "a preacher of righteousness" (II Peter 2:5), and he refers to this construction phase as a period "when God waited patiently in the days of Noah while the ark was being built." (I Peter 3:20) We can easily envision Noah, standing at the site of the construction of the ark, preaching of the coming judgment of God and offering the other inhabitants of earth an opportunity to repent and be saved. I remind you of the principle that God never allows a curse to fall without a warning. Unfortunately, no one in Noah's era heeded that warning.

One week before the point of no return had arrived, God told Noah to load the ark with his family and all the animals. He revealed that in 7 days He would send rain on the earth for 40 days and 40 nights. Noah was obedient, and when that day arrived God Himself shut the door to the ark behind Noah, then the rains began to fall.

Now 40 days and nights of torrential rain would probably cause horrendous wide spread flooding across parts of the earth. But it would not be enough to inundate the entire planet. Genesis 7:11 indicates that two other sources of water fed the deluge: "...on that day all the springs of the great deep burst forth, and the floodgates of heaven were opened." What were these "springs of the great deep" and "floodgates of heaven?"

Let's look first at the "springs of the great deep." The Hebrew word translated "deep" in the original text, is understood as meaning primarily subterranean waters, but it also denotes the sea, and the primeval ocean depths. We're somewhat familiar today with deep underground rivers, though it would seem their pre-flood counterparts were much larger, and deeper beneath the surface. We're familiar too, with seas and ocean depths. Again, however; we must bear in mind that these primeval seas and ocean depths were significantly different from those we presently know.

Something geologically momentous had to happen to cause these reservoirs to "burst forth." It's likely that massive earthquakes and/or volcanic eruptions triggered this hydraulic explosion. That kind of activity would probably also have resulted in massive uplifting of the ocean beds and transformation of the dry land. It may even have initiated the division of the dry ground into the continents as we now define them. And since up to 70% of what is spewed into the atmosphere by volcanoes today is water (mostly in the form of steam), this volcanic activity would have increased the magnitude of the flood as well.

The "floodgates of heaven" is considered by some as simply a reference to the rain clouds. But there's ample reason to believe something much more noteworthy is behind this phrase. Many scholars think the "floodgates of heaven" in Genesis 7:11 is synonymous with "the waters above it [that is, above the expanse, sky, or atmosphere]*" portrayed in the creation account in Genesis 1:6,7. As with "the floodgates of heaven," some consider "the waters above it," to be a reference to rain clouds.

But the description in the context seems to demand something far more extraordinary. "God said 'Let there be an expanse between the waters to separate water from water.' So God made the expanse and separated the water under the expanse from the water above it. And it was so. God called the expanse 'sky...'" Genesis 1:6-8) Separating the water *above* from the water *below*, at the very least *implies* that the waters above were more distinctive and substantial than scattered puffy or wispy clouds.

Based upon this and other evidences, many Christian men of science are convinced that there was a pre-flood water vapor or ice canopy above the atmosphere. This canopy, or "floodgates of heaven," may have been "opened" by the volcanic eruptions which would have exploded with tremendous force many miles into the sky. As we'll learn in the next chapter, the breakup of the canopy would not only have added to the floodwaters, but would have produced a radical change in our environment.

Incredibly swollen by the 40 days and nights of rain, the bursting forth of the springs of the great deep, and the opening of the floodgates of heaven, the floodwaters rose and lifted the ark and all its passengers off the ground. The waters continued to rise until they "covered the mountains to a depth of more than 20 feet." (Genesis 7:20) Ultimately "Everything on dry ground that had the breath of life in its nostrils died." (Genesis 7:22)

During this period, 8 human beings and thousands of animals survived a universal deluge by riding the waves in a massive wooden vessel. We're given no details of activities or conditions on the ark, so we can only make reasonable suppositions about what went on inside. Caring for that many creatures would certainly have kept Noah and his loved ones occupied during this unprecedented adventure. Feeding, watering, and disposing of waste would be a daunting responsibility.

In their comprehensive book on the subject, "The Genesis Flood," Doctors John C. Whitcomb and Henry M. Morris suggest a plausible means of shrinking this task. Dr. Whitcomb is a theology professor, and a recognized scholar on the Old Testament and the universal flood. Dr. Morris is a professor of hydraulic engineering, and served for many years as Chairman of the Civil Engineering Department of Virginia Polytechnic Institute and State University. He, too, is a noted authority on the flood.

In their book, they speculate that God may have caused the animals to enter into hibernation mode. In fact, since (as we'll learn in the next chapter) the pre-flood environment required no such thing as animal hibernation, this could have been the introduction of that process. In this dormant state, many of the animals would have required no food or water. Whatever the case, the passengers on the ark rode out the disaster in the safety of the ark God had designed, and Noah and his helpers had built.

Genesis chapter 8 begins by saying that God remembered all those in the ark, "and He sent a wind over the earth, and the waters receded." (Genesis 8:1) Eventually "the ark came to rest on the mountains of Ararat." (Genesis 8:4) Later the tops of other mountains became visible. In due course, Noah began sending out birds in an effort to determine if the ground was dry. He used a raven first, then on 3 subsequent occasions, a dove. The first 3 birds released returned. When the last dove did not come back to the ark, Noah knew the land was once again inhabitable. (Genesis 8:12) Approximately a year after the rains began, the whole surface of the ground was finally dry, and the Lord commanded Noah to disembark from the ark with his family and all the animals. Humans, animals, and the entire planet were on the threshold of a new beginning.

The first recorded act of Noah upon his return to dry ground was to worship God. In Genesis 8:20 we're informed that he "built an altar to the LORD... and sacrificed burnt offerings on it." As He always is, God was pleased with the worship, and out of His great heart He poured forth blessings. If we ever want to please God, it's vital we grasp the essence of worship. Physical actions of one kind or another are usually a part of worship. Noah built an altar and offered a sacrifice to the Lord. Nowadays Christians often tend to think of worship as doing "churchy" things like kneeling, bowing heads, singing hymns and choruses, raising or clapping hands, speaking or shouting words of praise, and even weeping or laughing.

These activities can be *part* of worship. But the *heart* of worship is the _heart_. Whatever our *deeds*, they fall completely short of worship unless they flow from deep within us. And it must be done God's way, not our way. In John 4:23, Jesus told an inquiring woman, "...true worshipers will worship the Father in *spirit* and *truth*, for these are the kind of worshipers the Father seeks." When our acts of devotion are done in accordance with God's Word (truth) and spring from our hearts (spirits), they are true worship. Worship flows from a heart that loves the Lord, and blessings flow from God the Father, to that human heart.

Not surprisingly, the Lord had chosen the right man with whom to start over. Once again He looked forward to *blessing*, rather than *cursing*, mankind. "The Lord smelled the pleasing aroma [of Noah's burnt offerings]* and said in His heart: 'Never again will I curse the ground because of man...'" (Genesis 8:21) God also said He would never again destroy all living creatures as he had. Then He blessed Noah and his sons, and established a covenant with them and all the animals, to never again destroy the earth with a flood. He sealed that covenant with an exquisite sign we have all seen in the sky at one time or another: a rainbow. (Genesis 9:13) It was a bright new beginning in a fresh and different world.

I see significant symbolism in that rainbow. And I believe that symbolism was intended by God. First, a rainbow requires *both* sunshine and rain to produce. Though we would prefer only the sunshine of good times, for us to appreciate the precious covenant relationship between the Lord and us in this post-Paradise, post-flood era, we also need the rain of hard times. The interaction of the two allows us a spectacular view of His love and care for us.

Secondly, science teaches us that the larger the

raindrops, the purer the colors of the rainbow. In other words, the heavier the rain of hard times, the richer the hues of this sign of God's covenant with us when the sunshine breaks through. We may not enjoy life's trials, but they afford us a clearer perception of God's ways. Thirdly, according to science no two people see the same rainbow exactly the same way, since its appearance is affected by the slightest variation in our point of view. So while we all can see God's rainbow, our different perspectives dictate that each of us sees a rainbow designed *just for us*.

Finally, there is such a thing as a *lunar* rainbow. If the full moon is bright enough, its light can also produce a rainbow, though that rainbow will not be as bright and colorful as one formed by the sun. Those of us who are God's children through having been born again, are reflections of God's glory, just as the moon is a reflection of the sun's glory. Through godly living, we too can generate a demonstration of God's covenant relationship for others to see.

At the outset of this discussion of the Genesis flood I asserted that "no other ancient narrative is buttressed by the records of so many disparate cultures and so much physical evidence." Before closing this chapter I want to offer you a small sampling of that supporting data.

Genesis does not contain the only testimony of a worldwide flood. Written and oral traditions of the deluge encircle the globe. The most well known of them outside of the Scriptures is the ancient Babylonian "Gilgamesh Epic." But there are literally scores of universal flood stories of lesser renown, and while the characters and other details vary, there are enough essential common elements in these stories to reflect unmistakably upon a common origin. Every account includes some kind of sin or immorality as the cause of the flood, one person receiving advanced warning of it, and the whole human population of the earth being wiped out... except for a handful of survivors. The vast majority of these narratives also mention that the survivors were spared through the use of some kind of water borne vessel. I'm convinced that the common source from which all these chronicles flow is *real history!*

One particularly interesting indication of the universality of the account of a worldwide flood is found in the words "flood" and "boat" in the Chinese language. Because the Chinese people were isolated from the rest of the world for so many millennia, we need to first remind ourselves that like all other ethnic groups, they share the same sites of origin: the Garden of Eden, the post-flood mountains of Ararat, and (as you'll discover in chapter 5 of this book) the tower of Babel.

With this understanding, we'll not be so surprised to find remarkable connections between certain characters in the written Chinese language and the events of the early chapters of the book of Genesis. Unlike written English, Chinese does not have 26 alphabetical letters from which words are created. It uses a single character to represent an entire word. Each of these characters is essentially a pictograph. What is so significant is that the characters for "eight," "united," and "earth" are joined to form one character for the word "*total*." Then the character for "*water*" is added to the character for "*total*" to finally form the composite character for "***flood***." Meanwhile the character for "***boat***" is a combination of the characters for "vessel," "eight," and "mouth."

It's not hard to see the correlation between these ancient Chinese characters for "*flood*" and "*boat*" and the Genesis account of the worldwide flood. We might express it this way: the eight members of Noah's family (representing eight mouths to feed) floated on the waters of the *flood* in the vessel or *boat* known as the ark, united as the total surviving human population of earth! Is the connection between these key Chinese words and the Genesis flood coincidental? I think not!

Having touched on the historical evidence provided through the many remarkably similar stories of a worldwide flood found in primitive ethnic traditions around the world, let's move on to the physical evidences for the authenticity of Noah's flood. The physical evidences of which I speak are geological in nature.

The most overwhelming confirmation of a universal deluge is that of the fossil beds. It may surprise you to discover that until the 19th century, fossil beds were universally believed by the western scientific community to be the result of the flood of Noah's day. This approach has changed over time since then, until today the prevailing view of the origin of the fossil beds is that most of them are the result of gradual sedimentary forces. According to this widely held opinion, some fossils may also be identified as the outcome of various other natural phenomena, but *none* ever attributed to a worldwide flood. This transformation of perspective is not, however, the result of any new scientific *fact* uncovered in the last couple of centuries. It's the product of a change in *theory*, and the introduction and ultimate prevalence of an anti-biblical bias.

More than any other man, a Scotsman (possessing, by the way, virtually no scientific education) named Charles

Lyell was responsible for this change in scientific opinion. Making rather rudimentary observations of the gradual sedimentary processes of rivers and lakes, and without using scientific methods, he determined that given enough time, these slow sedimentary actions better explained the fossil beds than did the Genesis deluge. Of course, this kind of proposal required the unfounded supposition of an earth many times older than the few thousand years indicated by the Bible.

Geologists who hold to the historical reality of a worldwide flood, concur that fossils are generally formed in sediment. However, they point out that very few fossils are found in the slow forming sediment of rivers and lakes, and that the molding of fossils usually requires the swift, turbulent action of powerful flood waters. For carcasses to be fossilized they must survive the normally rapid processes of scavenging by other animals and disintegration through decay. This fact argues for quick burial in water-borne sediment. Otherwise, few carcasses would survive intact to be fossilized.

The unfathomable number of fossils discovered all over the globe, their frequent concentrations in certain areas, and the curious location of some of those areas, prohibit the credible attributing of their development to gradual, non-catastrophic sedimentation. These vast deposits call for massive, extensive, raging avalanches of water, bringing a sudden end to living creatures. That animals are often buried together in large numbers indicates something huge abruptly overwhelmed them.

This is further evidenced by many fossilized remains of ancient creatures clearly manifesting the suddenness with which they died. One example of this suddenness is a display in the Princeton Museum of Natural History of the fossil of a perch in the act of eating a herring! And speaking of aquatic animals, there have been fossils of marine life found at elevations thousands of feet above any known past or present bodies of water, including shark and whale fossils in the Rocky Mountains! These can only be explained by the effects of a universal deluge.

The formation of coal beds and petroleum deposits would also seem to be verification of the universal deluge described in Genesis. Both coal and oil are organic in origin. And both are produced when that organic material is placed under great pressure. Evolutionists insist that this pressure was applied gradually over a period of millions of years. Yet experiments have shown that both coal and oil can be created under immense pressure in a very short time. And evolutionists have no adequate explanation for how the colossal volume of organic materials necessary to create the vast coal deposits and oil reservoirs gathered at these sites. The worldwide flood, with its sudden tremendous geologic upheaval and great sedimentary burial of dead animals and plants, is a better explanation for the existence of coal and oil than anything yet offered by flood skeptics.

A unique evidential monument to Noah's flood is located in the southwestern United States. I will never forget the moment I first stepped out onto the edge of the Grand Canyon. I had heard of it since childhood. I had seen it depicted in photos, movies, and on television. But nothing could have prepared me for the rush of sensations that swept over me in the instant I first beheld it. It's hard to describe what I felt. The magnitude of the chasm that lay before me far surpassed anything to which my memory could attempt to relate it. It was a vista without precedence. It nearly took my breath away. I can only imagine the reaction of the first Europeans to see it. Unlike me, they had no visual anticipation whatsoever to prime them for that moment. Their brains may have even attempted to deny the reality of what stretched out in front of them. This incredible geologic wonder extends for more than a hundred miles, and is at places a mile deep and 5 miles wide!

The stock evolutionary explanation for the origin of the Grand Canyon simply does not in my opinion hold water (pardon the pun!). The assertion that in the course of several million years the Colorado River cut through thousands of feet of sedimentary strata, which itself accumulated over a half billion years, is totally inadequate. It leaves many anomalies unaccounted for by its claim.

If, as this theory alleges, the strata was established through eons of environmental uplifts and downshifts, how do we explain the remarkable, almost perfectly uniform, horizontal consistency of this strata over a massive land area after ages of violent geologic upheaval? How do we account for the dramatic inconsistencies of the contents of this strata with the evolutionary geologic column? There have been many fossils, artifacts, etc. found in Grand Canyon strata that should be too old for those objects to have existed when that particular sedimentary strata was allegedly laid down. And how is it possible that the gorges supposedly created by the Colorado River are inconsistent with the universally observed character of river erosion? The principles of hydrodynamics dictate that water cannot meander horizontally at the same time as it's cutting deep vertically. Yet this is the very nature of the formations in the Grand Canyon!

Clearly, the most plausible explanation for the origin of the Grand Canyon is that it was formed in the wake of the worldwide flood. All of the above contradictions of evolutionary geology's theory are readily dealt with through accepting the historical reality of the deluge. Dr. John C. Whitcomb and Dr. Henry M. Morris give the gist of this perspective in two sentences in their book, "The Genesis Flood." In speaking of the stratagraphic layers of the walls of the Grand Canyon they state: "By far the most reasonable way of accounting for them is in terms of relatively rapid deposition out of the sediment-laden water of the Flood. Following the Flood, while the rocks were still comparatively soft and unconsolidated, the great canyons were rapidly scoured out as the waters rushed down from the newly-uplifted peneplains (nearly flat land surfaces representing an advanced stage of erosion)* to the newly-enlarged ocean basins."

Our discussion of some other geological evidences for the deluge will be reserved for the next chapter, where I'll detail some of the momentous differences between the antediluvian and postdiluvian worlds.

*Not in the original text. Added by the author for clarification.

CHAPTER 5

The Post-Flood World

" **B**ut they deliberately forget that long ago by God's word the heavens existed and the earth was formed out of water and by water. By these waters also *the world of that time was deluged and destroyed.* By the same word the present heavens and earth are reserved for fire, being kept for the day of judgment and destruction of ungodly men." With these words from II Peter 3:5-7, the Apostle makes it clear that there is a conspicuous difference between the pre-flood and post-flood worlds. He describes the former as "the world *of that time*" and the latter as "the *present* heavens and earth." He also hints at a new heaven and new earth yet to come. But I'll speak more of that in chapter 8. The point here is that the post-flood world in which we now live is both figuratively and literally poles apart from the one that preceded it. Even as our planet had changed dramatically after the Edenic curse, another dramatic change resulted from the curse of the worldwide flood. In this chapter we'll take a look at some of the major ways in which life on earth was altered radically by the deluge.

Let's begin with a noteworthy declaration made by God at the beginning of this post-flood era. "As long as the earth endures, seedtime and harvest, cold and heat, summer and winter, day and night will never cease." (Genesis 8:22). At first glance this would seem to be a promise of the *continuity* of environmental conditions which we might assume had already existed for a long time. But upon closer examination, we discover that most of these features of earthly life we now take for granted had never been mentioned prior to the deluge.

Further analysis will disclose that these conditions were likely *new* to Noah and his family. Even the alternating of day and night, which had been appointed by God in the beginning (Genesis 1:5), may have functioned differently in the pre-flood world, as I'll explain later. All of the other conditions listed in this passage, relate to the changing seasons as we now know them. But they were not spoken of previously in the Bible. Nor had there been any indication of rain falling (Genesis 7:4) or wind blowing (Genesis 8:1) until the flood. As we dig deeper, a likely rationale as to why the earlier Scriptures may have been silent on these matters will emerge.

A good starting point for this investigation would be a few verses introduced to you in the last chapter. Let's look again at Genesis 1:6,7, and this time we'll continue through verse 8. "And God said, 'Let there be an expanse between the waters to separate water from water.' So God made the expanse and separated the water under the expanse from the water above it. And it was so. God called the expanse 'sky.'" This work of God on the second day of creation is often assumed to apply to a division between earthly bodies of water (oceans, seas, rivers, lakes, etc.) and the clouds as we know them today, which consist of water vapor.

However, these "waters" above the "expanse," or sky, must have been very different from the puffy clouds scattered through our present atmosphere. Genesis 2:5,6 is part of an addendum to the account of the creation introduced in chapter 1, and adds this intriguing information: "...for the Lord God had not sent rain on the earth and there was no man to work the ground, but streams came up from the earth and watered the whole surface of the ground." Genesis 2:10 further explains: "A river watering the garden flowed from Eden; from there it was separated into four headwaters."

The implication is that earth's greenery was watered *not* by rain, but by underground rivers and streams which flowed up to the surface. This inference that there was no rain in the pre-flood world is further strengthened by the fact that the rainbow, given to Noah as a sign of the Lord's covenant, was evidently something *new*. Noah had almost certainly never seen a rainbow before. Since rainbows require sun and rain, and we know that the sun existed prior to the flood, then it logically follows that rain must have been absent in that primeval environment. Yet another clue to this understanding is provided in Hebrews 11:7, where it tells us that "By faith, Noah, when warned about *things not seen*, in holy fear built an ark to save his family." What were the "things not seen" of which Noah was warned? It likely refers to the flood, and the mechanisms that triggered it, including rain. In all probability none of these had ever been seen or experienced by the people of Noah's time.

Concerning the flood waters, I previously pointed out

that the Bible informs us that a major source of these flood waters was "the floodgates of the heavens" that "were opened." (Genesis 7:11) Scientists have calculated that if all the rain clouds in our entire atmosphere were to disperse their rain at once, it would only be enough to accumulate less than an inch of additional water worldwide. And that process would take less than a day, *not* the 40 days and nights cited in Genesis 7:12. So it seems highly unlikely that these "floodgates of heaven" were simply clouds as we currently recognize them. What then, were the *waters above the sky* or *floodgates of heaven*, and what effect would they have had on life on earth? A penetrating inquiry into those questions will open for us a most fascinating subject.

Christian men of science who've researched the scriptural data about this issue, and the physical evidences relating to it, have come to a conclusion widely acknowledged among those researching these matters. They believe a huge, transparent or translucent canopy of water in some form (most commonly thought to be vapor) completely surrounded the planet until the time of the worldwide flood. Because no one from the pre-flood era is around to tell us, since the Bible gives us little detail about these waters above the expanse, and because no other written records from that time have been found relating to the topic, this proposal lies in the realm of theory. But it is a theory consistent with the Bible account, and many known facts about the earth.

Intriguingly, astronauts aboard the International Space Station reported seeing shiny, silvery blue clouds in the upper atmosphere where clouds do not normally exist. These clouds are thought to be the product of volcanic ash particles serving as hosts to icy water vapor. Yet their very existence points towards the viability of an ancient water vapor canopy high above the earth.

Even scientists who do not endorse the canopy theory, acknowledge that radically changing water vapor levels could have contributed to the sudden climatic changes which occurred millennia ago. Scientific study on the matter continues, so many details have yet to be nailed down. And there are noteworthy variations on this water canopy theory. But enough has been established for me to present you with some pertinent and captivating information.

It's been scientifically proven that such a canopy would produce a greenhouse effect on earth. Warm temperatures would prevail over the entire globe, with no major variation from one place to another. A greater portion of the sun's energy would be absorbed and maintained by this canopy, and thus be more evenly distributed over the planet. In addition, once absorbed by the ground, less of this energy and heat would be able to escape the atmosphere. Such conditions would produce a universally warm subtropical environment. There would be no extreme cold at the north and south poles.

The idea that such climatic conditions at one time existed at the poles is bolstered by the fact that fossil-bearing coal seams have been unearthed in Antarctica. These deposits consist of the transformed remains of vegetation which would be unable to survive in the current climate. How did this vegetation get there? Obviously, at one time conditions in Antarctica supported its growth! Numerous skeletons of animals which could only survive in a warm climate also have been uncovered in the frozen continent. Similar astounding finds have been documented in the Arctic region as well. The remains of a 90 foot plum tree with green leaves and ripe fruit was discovered in the far north New Siberian Islands, and evidence of tropical plants and trees have been found in Alaska. This is only a short list of similar findings at the northern and southern extremes of our planet. All of this information adds credibility to the water canopy theory.

Such a canopy would also increase atmospheric pressure, and levels of carbon dioxide and oxygen. And in fact, scientific testing of ancient air bubbles trapped in amber (a pale yellow, sometimes reddish or brownish, fossil resin of vegetable origin), have indicated there was once considerably more oxygen in the atmosphere than there is currently, perhaps as much as 50% more. This environment would promote remarkable growth of both plants and animals. The canopy would also serve as a barrier to harmful radiation and ultraviolet rays from the sun. Add to that the beneficial consequences of the stronger magnetic field that science has demonstrated would have been in force thousands of years ago, and you have pre-flood conditions on earth far more favorable to life, growth, and health than at present.

And there is significant evidence of just such life favorable conditions in both the Bible and the fossil record. As pointed out in chapter 3, the average life span of those listed in the pre-flood genealogy was more than 9 centuries. Also, human footprints in stone, so large that scientists have estimated the height of those who left them to be in excess of 8 feet, have been excavated in the bed of the Paluxy River in Texas. In September of 2003, "Science" magazine reported the discovery in northern Venezuela, of the fossil of a huge rodent believed to be related to our modern day guinea pig. It was roughly the size of a buffalo! But these are not isolated finds. Archeology has revealed that many ancient animals and plants would dwarf their contemporary counterparts.

One of the more fascinating changes brought about by a collapse of the water canopy is alluded to in the story of Noah's drunken stupor in the latter verses of Genesis chapter 9. This incident seems out of character with the Bible's pronouncement that "Noah was a righteous man, blameless among the people of his time, and he walked with God." (Genesis 6:9) While it is a fact that righteous people are still capable of falling into sin on occasions, many scholars believe that Noah might not have known that this post-flood wine would intoxicate him.

The text recounting the incident is worded in such a way as to suggest that his drunkenness was not anticipated by Noah or his sons. Two factors could have contributed to his naiveté. The pre-flood canopy would have diminished the sun's radiation, and that radiation is an important contributor to the fermentation process. Thus, it may have been that grape juice could not have developed significant alcohol content before the deluge. Additionally, the higher atmospheric pressure under the canopy would have minimized the human body's metabolism of alcohol, thus inhibiting intoxication prior to the flood. Not only was this the first account of drunkenness in the Bible, it might well have been the first incidence of intoxication in history. Drunkenness could very well be one more upshot of the curse of the worldwide flood.

One of the scientists espousing a variation on the water canopy theory is Dr. Carl Baugh. He believes

God created this canopy out of the two elements which comprise water: hydrogen and oxygen. He contends that the "water under the expanse" spoken of in Genesis 1:7 was not the earthly bodies of water such as the ocean, but the lower portion of 2 composite layers of water encasing another expanse within it. In his estimation, the biblical context makes this clear. Dr. Baugh calls attention to the fact that the Hebrew word for "expanse" in Genesis 1:6-8 means "to compress or pound out."

Dr. Baugh then references an experiment carried out some years back at the Lawrence Livermore National Laboratories. There the elements of water were compressed in cryogenic cold. Under those conditions hydrogen took on a nearly metallic nature, becoming "crystalline, transparent, fiber optic, super conductive, and ferromagnetic." There is much more to his theory, but the bottom line is that he proposes a canopy 11 miles above the earth, consisting of compressed metallic hydrogen in the middle of a solid water formation. Among the unique effects of this formation would be a variant day/night cycle, and a far different color to the sky. Dr. Baugh says: "At high noon there would have been a light pink coloration in the sky; at sunrise and sunset there would have been a vivid pink coloration; and at midnight there would have been a magenta pink sky. In other words, the sky before the flood was never totally dark."

As Director of the Creation Evidences Museum in Glen Rose, Texas, Dr. Baugh designed and supervised the construction and operation of a hyper baric biosphere chamber intended to recreate the conditions of the pre-flood environment. Animals kept in this chamber have undergone striking transformations. Among the results are fruit flies living up to 3 times longer than normal, the growth of piranha fish accelerating from 2 inches to 16 inches over a 2.5 year period, and the venom of poisonous copperhead snakes reverting to a non-toxic state. His experiments have indicated conditions on earth prior to the opening of "the floodgates of heaven" would have been vastly more conducive to long and healthy life than those of the present.

This life enhancing setting was lost to the curse of sin, delivered through the worldwide flood. In its place a whole new environment developed. The effects of the process of decay, which began with the curse that followed the sin of Adam and Eve, were accelerated by the extension of that curse through the deluge. In particular, the demise of the radiation and ultraviolet shielding provided by the water canopy would have led to many diseases and premature aging. Health and longevity suffered, while sickness and death prospered. Gradually, average life expectancy dropped from nearly a millennium to less than a century. A modern post-flood person's average life span is about 8% of that of our pre-flood ancestors.

Rapid environmental transition in the aftermath of the worldwide flood introduced spectacular climate changes on earth, with the initiation of cold temperatures and all the associated ramifications. The development of the ice enshrouded north and south poles, as well as the historical period commonly known as the ice age, can logically trace their origins to the immediate aftermath of the deluge.

Following the collapse of the great water dome, modern weather conditions were ushered into the global arena. The loss of uniformly distributed heat, owing to the departure of the canopy's greenhouse effect was the first of these mechanisms of change. The ensuing development of the water cycle with its principles of evaporation and precipitation, and the establishment of atmospheric disturbances featuring various wind patterns, would also be among the catalysts establishing earth weather as we now know it.

You see, in the absence of the canopy, the differences in heat generation between the more direct sunlight near the equator and the less direct sunlight at the poles, allowed for the creation of the polar ice caps, and initiated the ice age. Snow began to fall in the more distant regions of the northern and southern hemispheres. This precipitation was likely far greater than at any time during the present age, due to the high volumes of volcanic ash probably present in the post-flood atmosphere. Over the course of time, much ocean water was displaced to the poles through this process, forming massive ice caps. These glacial structures probably spread closer to the equator until they reached latitudes and altitudes at which temperatures in summer began to melt them.

Summer, of course, along with winter, spring, and fall, became pronounced seasons without the temperature mitigating effects of the former water canopy. The winds began to carry weather fronts across the face of the earth. In this post-flood era extreme weather in the form of violent storms such as hurricanes, tornadoes, blizzards, and torrential rains with the ensuing floods, have brought death to millions. These deaths then, are ultimately a result of the curse of sin implemented through the deluge.

Before we move on, I want to call to your attention some of the additional consequences wrought upon the animal kingdom by the climatic changes resulting from the loss of the water canopy. Many animals would have had to embrace new lifestyles in this transformed climate. Some located permanently to tropical or sub-tropical areas of the world. Certain species of birds began to migrate seasonally to various parts of the earth to avoid the cold weather and its ramifications. A number of mammals, reptiles, amphibians, and fish in temperate regions developed hibernation abilities. Some established ways to store food internally or externally for the winter. Other mammals in yet colder areas added additional fur and fat for the winter to protect themselves from the extreme temperatures. Those who would not or could not adapt, eventually became extinct.

One animal group that may have become extinct in the wake of the flood was the dinosaurs. There are a number of theories as to their disappearance. One plausible scenario is that most of them were simply unable to adapt to the new post-flood environment. Atmospheric changes could have made it difficult for many dinosaurs with relatively small lung capacity to provide their huge bodies with the amount of oxygen they needed. That would have left only smaller dinosaur types such as alligators, crocodiles, caimans, and komodo dragons able to survive. Although, based on reports of sightings in remote tropical areas of the globe, some scientists believe that a few larger species of dinosaurs may still survive in minute numbers to this very day.

Besides climatic changes, extensive topographic shifts were brought about by the flood. And these topographic modifications would also play a role in aspects of the new weather systems. Specifically, I'm speaking of the re-shaped oceans and uplifted mountain ranges which influence current weather conditions. The same earthquakes and volcanic eruptions which likely caused "all the springs of the great deep" to "burst forth" (Genesis 7:11) would have wreaked havoc with the earth's crust. I touched on this subject briefly in the previous chapter.

Doctors John C. Whitcomb and Henry M. Morris have pointed to Psalm 104:5-9 as a Bible account of this geologic event. This Scripture passage reads as follows: "He established the earth upon its foundations, so that it will not totter forever and ever. Thou didst cover it with the deep as with a garment; the waters were standing above the mountains. At Thy rebuke they fled; at the sound of Thy thunder they hurried away. The mountains rose; the valleys sank down to the place Thou didst establish for them. Thou didst set a boundary that they may not pass over; that they may not return to cover the earth." (NASB Bible)

That this passage does not simply refer to the original creation, but instead to the deluge, is evidenced by two facts. First, the original oceans did not cover *previously existing* mountains. Second, and more importantly, the last sentence in this passage essentially repeats God's promise to Noah that He would never again destroy the whole world with water. That "the mountains rose" indicates a heightening past their previous altitudes. That the mountains were formerly lower would also mean that less water would be required to cover them during the flood. And following Noah's flood "the valleys sank down" to provide a deeper ocean basin than before. This would be necessary for them to hold the additional waters which had come to the surface of the earth during the flood.

Some years ago German scientist, Alfred Wegener, proposed that today's continents once formed a single land mass. He suggested that due to the weaknesses in the earth's crust, it gradually separated over millions of years into the continents as we know them today. This has been called "continental drift." There is some plausible evidence that all our continents may have been part of one super continent in the past. If the core of this theory is true, then the flood and its accompanying seismic activity could have been the mechanism by which the bulk of this massive movement took place in a matter of months... not millions of years. And it may very well be that this cataclysmic rearrangement of the earth's crust became the source of the instability which generates earthquakes, tsunamis and volcanic eruptions. If so (and this seems likely), then the costly destruction and tragic loss of life resulting from these natural disasters must be added to the list of earth's troubles attributable to the curse.

The last of the major changes from the pre-flood to post-floods worlds to which I want to call your attention are found in Genesis 9:2-6, where God says to human beings: "The fear and dread of you will fall upon all the beasts of the earth and all the birds of the air, upon every creature that moves along the ground, and upon all the fish of the sea; they are given into your hands. Everything that lives and moves will be food for you. Just as I gave you the green plants, I now give you everything. But you must not eat meat that has its lifeblood in it. And for your lifeblood I will surely demand an accounting. I will demand an accounting from every animal. And from each man, too, I will demand an accounting for the life of his fellow man. Whoever sheds the blood of man, by man shall his blood be shed; for in the image of God has God made man." Here, momentous issues of fear, food, life and death are dealt with by the Lord.

These alterations began with a further blow, extending beyond that of the Edenic curse, to the harmony that originally existed among all creatures on earth. After Adam and Eve sinned, an animal had to die to provide a covering for their nakedness. Antagonism was established between humans and snakes. Now the "fear and dread" of man was to fall upon all the animals. You may remember that in Genesis 2:19,20 we're told that God brought all the land animals to Adam. Not only was this an opportunity for Adam to name them, but for the Lord and/or Adam to find a suitable "helper" for the first man from among the animals.

The very suggestion that a human could look for close companionship among these creatures reveals a certain level of camaraderie which had already existed. We have a pale modern parallel to the benefits of that primeval friendship in the studies which have documented the positive impact pets have on their owners. The presence of pets usually promotes family closeness, warmth, more healthy playing, and less arguing. Researchers have found that high blood pressure is reduced, "feel-good" hormones are released, and lifespan is increased by the company our animal friends. Domestic pets taken to elderly group homes bring smiles to the faces of the lonely. If this much good flows from the relationship between humans and their pets today, imagine how much we might benefit from that kind of camaraderie with the entire animal kingdom! But alas, the fall of mankind in Paradise began a process of the degeneration of that fellowship between man and animal. And after the deluge it disintegrated into a widespread mutual distrust. Though not explicitly expressed here, it seems likely that this same corruption of relationships was occurring among the animals themselves.

The highly respected 18th century Bible commentator, Matthew Henry, draws our attention to the similarity and dissimilarity between Genesis 1:28 and Genesis 9:2, the latter being part of the passage quoted two pages earlier. In the former, God tells Adam and Eve: "Rule over... every living creature." In the latter, God speaks to Noah and his sons, and says of all the animals: "The fear and dread of you will fall upon all... they are given into your hands." Matthew Henry declares this latter word, giving man dominion over the animals after the flood, "...revives a former grant... only with this difference, that man in *innocence* ruled by *love, fallen* man rules by *fear.*" What a sad distinction!

Noah and all his descendents (including you and me) were from now on permitted by God to eat the meat of animals. It logically follows that animals also were probably allowed to become carnivorous at the same time. This is not to say with certainty that humans never ate animals, and animals never ate other animals or humans prior to this. We only know for sure that the Lord gave mankind *permission* to eat animals *after* the flood. It could be that Abel may have eaten meat in connection with his offering of "fat portions" from some of his flock. It's possible that individual humans were granted permission to eat animal flesh before the flood. It's also possible that men consumed meat without God's general approval. And it could be that some animals were already becoming meat eaters, though the fact that Scripture offers no record of inter-animal conflicts while boarding or living aboard the ark, would seem to argue against such. As to exactly when men and animals became carnivores, and whether that transition was sudden or gradual, we can only speculate. But it is clear that the deluge marked a turning point, and God now permitted men to kill and eat animals.

But with this newly approved action came a restriction pregnant with meaning: "But you must not eat meat that has its lifeblood still in it." (Genesis 9:4) The immediate understanding of this command seems to involve a degree of kindness to the animals over whom God had reaffirmed man's authority. It would prohibit humans from undo cruelty to the creatures whose very lives were providing food for them. Men must not (as some animals do with one another) consume animals alive, or cut off a limb to eat it, while leaving the animal to suffer.

But this command was also the herald of a broader comprehension of the significance of blood. The Law of Moses, and later, the crucifixion of Jesus Christ, would further clarify the worth God has placed on life and sacrificial death. In an age when we simply go supermarket shopping for meat, most of us have little appreciation for the sacrificial death of animals. Many years ago when I was pastoring a church in Connecticut, a parishioner shared an insight which has stayed with me. She and her husband had drastically changed lifestyle, exchanging suburbia for a farm. The first time they slaughtered livestock for food was an awakening for them. The wife told me that at that moment she fully realized that through the shedding of its blood, the animal was literally giving its life for her and her family. The spiritual implications of that experience were powerful.

This new era of history also introduced the divine authorization of the death penalty. In Genesis 9:5,6 the Lord says: "And for your lifeblood I will surely demand an accounting. I will demand an accounting from every animal. And from each man, too, I will demand an accounting for the life of his fellow man. Whoever sheds the blood of man, by man shall his blood be shed; for in the image of God has God made man."

The first murder, when Cain killed his brother Abel, evoked a curse and a punishment from God. Cain's career as a farmer was ruined, and he was driven out of the Lord's presence and became a "restless wanderer" on the earth (Genesis 4:11-14). But the Lord did not take Cain's life. In fact, the Lord prohibited any other human being from killing Cain (Genesis 4:15). In the wake of the deluge however; God instituted capital punishment for both man and beast. I suspect that the Creator did this in an effort to discourage a return to the violent culture which had precipitated the worldwide flood. Contrary to the opinion of some, the death penalty is not a *devaluation* of human life, but an affirmation of it's immense *value* in the eyes of God. His validation for authorizing the act of one human executing another human as sentence for murder is "...for in the image of God has God made man." (Genesis 9:6) The fact that God fashioned man in His own likeness is the true basis of the sanctity of life.

In the aftermath of the flood, Noah and his family were blessed by the Lord, and commanded to "Be fruitful and increase in number and fill the earth." (Genesis 9:1) This is essentially the same command given to humanity in

Genesis 1:28: "God blessed them and said to them, 'Be fruitful and increase in number, fill the earth and subdue it.'" That parallel is not surprising, since just as Adam and Eve commenced the expansion of the first human population of the planet; Noah, his wife, and family, were by God's design starting that process all over again.

Even as all mankind in the pre-flood world traced their lineage from one man and one woman, so all of us in the post-flood era are descended from yet another solitary couple. Scientific study in the field of genetics has proved that fact. Mitochondrial DNA connects all of humanity ancestrally as the offspring of a solitary woman. In fact, some scientific calculations based upon the mutation rate of mitochondrial DNA, place the mother of all mankind on the planet about 6,000 years ago. That date is very much in line with Bible-based estimates of the beginning of time, and presents a dilemma to evolutionary theory, since that hypothesis has declared the origin of humanity to be *millions* of years ago.

Genesis chapter 10 records the initial fulfillment of the divine edict to "fill the earth," tracing the descendents of Noah and his sons. This genealogy is commonly referred to as "The Table of Nations." It provides the origins of the nations and races of the world, and has been hailed by some professional archeologists and anthropologists as the most valuable and accurate resource available in that area of research.

In the course of this extensive genealogy, particular attention is given to Nimrod, whose ungodly leadership was apparently the catalyst for a key crisis in the ongoing saga of fallen humanity. His very name is a sign of his character. Nimrod means: "the rebel." Genesis 10:8 says he "...grew to be a mighty warrior on the earth." The Hebrew word translated "mighty warrior" is derived from a root word meaning: "to rise, to be greater, stronger, to prevail, overwhelm." Nimrod managed to prevail over many of the other inhabitants of his time. Most of his fellowmen were content with equality. The rebel Nimrod's ambition was to rise above his fellow man, and as we will see, to even rise above his Maker. Noah's path to prominence was his humble submission to God. Nimrod's ascendance was the fruit of his selfish, rebellious aspirations. God honored Noah. Nimrod honored himself.

Nimrod was the forerunner of all self-made men, the father of all worship-craving dictators. He built cities and ruled from them, establishing his empire across a broader and broader segment of humanity. Since Nimrod was also a "mighty hunter" (Genesis 10:9), it's been speculated that he may have secured the loyalty and submission of his subjects by hunting down ferocious beasts and constructing walled cities to protect those people he ruled over from such danger. Though not as authoritative as Scripture, there are extra-biblical Jewish and Christian writings which tell us a little more about Nimrod. Of particular interest is an assertion in the writings of the church fathers that, aided by demonic power, Nimrod led the people into the false religion of astrology. This astrology connection is supported by Isaiah 47:13, which speaks of the powerful and detrimental influence of Babylon's astrologers.

Babylon, of course, was the first center of Nimrod's kingdom. (Genesis 10:10) And it was there, likely under his leadership, that the crisis, to which I alluded a few paragraphs ago, arose. The event is chronicled in Genesis

11:1-9: "Now the whole world had one language and a common speech. As men moved eastward, they found a plain in Shinar, and settled there. They said to each other, 'Come, let's make bricks and bake them thoroughly.' They used brick instead of stone, and tar for mortar. Then they said, 'Come, let us build ourselves a city, with a tower that reaches to the heavens, so that we may make a name for ourselves and not be scattered over the face of the whole earth.' But the LORD came down to see the city and the tower that the men were building. The LORD said, 'If as one people speaking the same language they have begun to do this, then nothing they plan to do will be impossible for them. Come, let us go down and confuse their language so they will not understand each other.' So the LORD scattered them from there over all the earth, and they stopped building the city. That is why it was called Babel -- because there the LORD confused the language of the whole world. From there the LORD scattered them over the face of the whole earth."

The tower they were constructing has been identified by many scholars as an ancient stepped pyramid structure known as a "ziggurat." The ziggurat seems to have symbolized a connection between heaven and earth. It supposedly was provided for the gods to use in their travel from the one realm to the other. In the pagan Mesopotamian culture which was developing in that period, urban leaders (including perhaps Nimrod himself) were often deified, so the ziggurat provided them access to heaven. Ziggurats have frequently been connected with astrology. This links very nicely with the conviction of the church fathers that Nimrod led his people into astrology.

Until that moment in history everyone spoke the same

God-given language as did Adam and Eve. It was a benefit bestowed by the Creator. But any benefit can become a detriment once sin begins its corrosive work. And the pride and rebellion of Nimrod had seeped into the lives of his followers. Together they determined not to glorify God, but themselves. They wanted to make a name for themselves rather than exalt the name of the Lord.

Their sin was of the very same nature as that of Adam and Eve prior to them, and the devil and his cohorts even before that. They were making idols of their ruler and themselves. Knowing the disastrous consequences of that idolatry to humanity, God had to act. His action at the Tower of Babel was essentially the same as it was in the Garden of Eden. The benefit of a common language now turned detriment, had to be recalled. In the Garden access to the Tree of Life was cancelled. At the Tower of Babel common speech had to be brought to an end. Otherwise man's awesome potential, combined with his unholy unity, would multiply his evil deeds and achievements. The Lord confused their languages and scattered them around the world.

Some Bible scholars also believe that God forcibly scattered humans at this time because, by gathering in a large city in order "not be scattered over the face of the whole earth," (Genesis 11:4) they were in direct disobedience to His command to Noah's descendents to "fill the earth." (Genesis 9:1) Why might the Lord not want people to congregate in large cities? Think for a few moments and the answers may become self-evident.

Dense population centers make it easy for would-be tyrants to manipulate the masses. On a sin-cursed planet, the potential societal benefits of shared resources in a mammoth community, are easily perverted into hoarded personal wealth and tyranny by the greedy and power hungry. Large, closely housed populations are more vulnerable to dictators like Nimrod. Also, the same collective colony which can share and multiply good, under the powerful influence of the sin nature frequently becomes a breeding ground for evil. And ask yourself, where is the crime rate higher... in rural areas and villages, or big cities? Maybe there is some real merit to the interpretation that *spreading out* was what God meant when He commanded mankind to "fill the earth."

The historicity of this Scriptural incident in Babylon on the plain of Shinar has inadvertently gained some support from scientific research into linguistic origins. The March 1990 Scientific American magazine printed an article on a study seeking to discover the source of various European languages. A previous investigation had postulated that European languages developed in Europe. But the study cited in this issue of Scientific American concluded that European languages actually began in the Middle East. Once again, the Bible is proving itself to be a uniquely reliable source of history.

The events at, and leading up to the tower of Babel, so soon after the entire population (Noah and his family) had known and acknowledged their Creator, display an unfortunate pattern of behavior repeated throughout human history. Romans 1:18-32 outlines this paradigm in substantial detail. It's a pattern first seen in the Garden of Eden, then observed again after mankind's expulsion from there. It recurred after the worldwide flood. And it has been repeated over and over again by communities and nations across the earth. You'll find it encapsulated in Romans 1:21: "For although they knew God, they neither glorified him as God nor gave thanks to him, but their thinking became futile and their foolish hearts were darkened." Fallen humanity is naturally inclined to slide from a starting point of faith in God, to foolish paganism.

Could it be that what happened to those early Babylonians was in some way a precursor of what has since happened to other advanced societies who have so exceedingly rejected God's principles? Could the ancient Mayans, Minoans, and others have mysteriously disappeared from history in a similar manner? Has the Lord had to save humanity from itself on other such occasions? In the entire history of the world, God's judgment has never been an end in itself. Every judgment of the Lord has invariably been succeeded by a new beginning.

We might think that after humans had confirmed their implacable infidelity through three major failures (in the eras of Adam, Noah, and Nimrod), the Lord would have destroyed them once and for all! But He is a God of mercy and grace. He pursues His eternal purposes for mankind with amazing patience. Following the failure at Babylon, God continued reaching out to establish a relationship with these wayward creatures... a relationship through which He could fully extend His blessings to them. The curse seemed to be tightening its grip on the earth. Yet in love, the Lord pressed on with his plan to find a nation, a community, a family, or even one single person with whom He could share His great heart.

CHAPTER 6

Two Covenants

Previously, we've only briefly mentioned the term "covenant." Now we're going to take a closer look at this vital Bible concept. The word "covenant" first appears in Scripture in Genesis 6:17,18. There God told Noah that after destroying the earth through the worldwide flood, He would establish a covenant with Noah and his family. That same covenant is elaborated on in Genesis 9:8-17, where the Lord makes it clear that it would reach beyond Noah's family to also encompass *all* of earth's creatures.

There are numerous covenants in the Bible, particularly in the Old Testament. They involve God, men, and occasionally animals. Some are between God and people. Some, like the first one mentioned above, are between God and men and animals. And some are between people only. But three covenants *between God and men* stand above the rest. Two of them are the focus of this chapter: the Abrahamic Covenant and the Siniatic Covenant. Before dealing with these in detail, I need to explain what a covenant is.

Covenant as presented in Scripture is not a concept

readily familiar to moderns. The English word "covenant" does not convey the full sense of a true *biblical* covenant.

Other similar terms such as alliance, agreement, contract, pact, and treaty, also fall far short. The Hebrew word translated "covenant" throughout the Old Testament does lay a foundation for our understanding. It comes from a root word meaning "to fetter." Clearly, a covenant "fetters" or bonds two or more parties together. But the nature and manner of that bonding in a biblical covenant is unique... so unique that there is no single word or concept in English adequate to communicate it. The Spanish Bible translator, De Reyna, faced the same dilemma when rendering the Scripture into that language as well. He declared what was needed was a word which signified an agreement "made in conjunction with the ceremonial death of an animal." There was no such word in Spanish, and there is no such word in English.

A biblical covenant is a formal bonding of two or more parties, powerfully obligating one or more of them to certain stipulations. That commitment was so solemn that to break it would be considered high treason, generating dire consequences for such a breach. The sacrificial death of an animal at the sealing of the covenant, signified the solemnity of the relationship. This shedding of life blood was central to the covenant.

Other rites also often accompanied the covenant ceremony. Sometimes both parties walked between halves of the sacrificed animal. A meal might be shared. Hands would often be joined. There could be an exchange of gifts, and even an exchange of names, whereby each party added the name of the other to his own. A memorial may have been erected as a symbol and reminder of the agreement. All of these rites bound the parties to each other in covenant relationship for the rest of their lives.

A covenant could be *unilateral*, requiring specific obligations on the part of one, without a reciprocating responsibility on the part of the other. Or it could be *bilateral*, placing obligations and/or conditions on both parties. The two covenants discussed in this chapter represent one of each of these types. But both are covenants of the highest order on earth... covenants between *God and man.*

Why did God begin to covenant with man? No such covenant appears to have been made until *after* the worldwide flood. That fact could be the starting place for understanding the purpose of God's covenants with man. Before the flood, in the early period of humanity's existence on earth, Adam and Eve enjoyed a completely pure and innocent bond with the Creator. They lived in the full blessing of God. All they needed to know was either understood intuitively or communicated by the Lord face to face with them. Their relationship with Him was so uninhibited that they needed no verbal or written assurance to feel secure in it. Immediately after sin entered their lives, those innocent elements of mankind's intimacy with God were lost, and over time ebbed even further away.

By the time of the flood humanity had made itself the avowed enemy of God. Then with the judgment of the deluge behind them, and a new beginning before them, the Lord saw fit to restore that relationship and its benefits through covenant with those who truly longed to know Him. Covenant would reinstate the blessing, communicate the provisions of their kinship, and provide a basis for faith in God's love for His people.

But as we learned in the last chapter, following the deluge and the subsequent covenant with Noah, people again began to turn away from the Lord. Still, in God's heart a plan for another reconciliation was already at work. Less than three centuries after the flood, a child who would one day become the progenitor of the Jewish people was born in idolatrous Ur of the Chaldeans in Mesopotamia. His reach however; would extend far beyond the resultant people of Israel. The nature of his relationship with the Almighty is marked by some of the expressions through which the Bible would ultimately describe him: "the man of faith," (Galatians 3:9) "a father of many nations," (Genesis 17:5, Romans 4:17) and "God's friend." (James 2:23) Before he reached 50 years of age, humanity would once more be in outright rebellion against their Maker at the Tower of Babel. And yet, again God would be seeking someone with whom He could have intimate fellowship, and through whom he could pursue His original desire to bless all mankind. The Lord found that person in this lone Chaldean man. His name was Abram. What initially drew God to this person? The Bible does not directly tell us, but as we'll see, Abram's story hints at things about him that drew the Lord to him.

The record of the call of Abram into this special divine relationship begins in the first 3 verses of Genesis chapter 12: "The Lord had said to Abram, 'Leave your country, your people and your father's household and go to the land I will show you. I will make you into a great nation and I will bless you; I will make your name great and you will be a blessing. I will bless those who bless you, and whoever curses you I will curse; and all peoples on earth will be blessed through you.'"

Earlier verses from the latter part of Genesis chapter 11 inform us that Terah (Abram's father), Abram, Abram's nephew, Lot, and their families all had departed from Ur on a journey to Canaan. But the divine declaration to Abram quoted above had occurred prior to that extended household expedition. According to Acts 7:2, the call of God had been initially received by Abram while he was still in Mesopotamia, *before* he had moved to Haran. That's why Genesis 12:1 begins by stating in the *past tense*: "The Lord *had said* to Abram..."

For some reason their journey from Mesopotamia to Canaan was interrupted and they settled in Haran. The reason for that disruption is not revealed in Scripture. Perhaps the infirmities of old age prevented Terah from traveling further. Or maybe Terah was too attached to Mesopotamia and its idolatry to leave it completely behind. In any event, it appears the call of God to Abram was repeated, as we quoted from Genesis 12:1-3, following Terah's death. By that time Abram was 75 years old. Though we are not explicitly told why God chose Abram, the next verse (Genesis 12:4) provides an indication: "So Abram left, as the LORD had told him..." God's friend was the kind of man who acted in *faith* and *obedience* to God's commands.

It's not coincidental that God's call to Abram spoke of blessings and cursings. The Almighty's purpose was to bless Abram and make him a channel of blessing to others. The Lord was starting over again with this righteous man, just as He had with Noah. God's desire was to overcome the curse and reestablish His righteous, loving rule over humanity *through* Abram. If Abram was to be *God's means* of blessing men, then men who cursed (or rejected) *God's means* would be cursed by God. (Genesis 12:3) In Genesis 18:19, the Lord declared of Abram: "For I have chosen him, so that he will direct his children and his household after him to keep the way of the LORD by doing what is right and just..." Abram was the foundation of a new race of people. A wonderful honor and responsibility was placed upon him. He was to direct his family and household (servants) in the way of the Lord by example and instruction. Through Abram would flow God's blessing or curse.

Abram's faith and obedience toward God were exhibited throughout his life. This man's faithfulness is introduced to us from the very start. Reared in an ungodly society, he resisted the magnetism of popular culture and the appeal of the self-gratifying ways of his peers. He was hungry for the true God and His ways. When God called, Abram was willing to exchange the familiar for the unknown. He was commanded by God to leave his country, his people, and his father's household. At the outset he was not even told what his final destination would be. The Lord had simply bid him to "go to the land *I will show you.*" (Genesis 12:1)

Abram's character shone through in episode after episode. When his spiritually immature nephew, Lot, paid the price for too cozy a relationship with wicked people, his uncle Abe came to the rescue. Lot and his family had been captured as prisoners of a war against his then hometown of Sodom. So Abram assembled 318 men from his own household and attacked and routed the armies of the four kings who had attacked that city. He not only liberated Lot, but all of his ungodly acquaintances and their possessions as well. When the grateful king of Sodom offered him a rich reward for his victory, Abram refused to accept it. Why? Because he had taken an oath before the Lord not to allow anyone else but God to be able to say "I made Abram rich." (Genesis 14:22-24)

Later, when the stench of evil from the twin cities of Sodom and Gomorrah reached such intolerable proportions that God was forced to rain down judgment on them, Abram interceded with God. He pleaded for the Lord to spare the cities for the sake of any righteous people who might live in them. His intercession ultimately saved the lives of the only godly persons to be found there: Lot and his family.

When God promised an aging, childless Abram that He would give him a son, and through that son innumerable descendents in the ages to come, Abram believed God against impossible odds. After that precious son of promise, Isaac, had miraculously arrived and had grown to perhaps the age of 12, Abram once more demonstrated his faithfulness to God. The Lord asked His friend to give that special son back to Him in sacrificial death. Abram not only obeyed, but believed God's promise enough to expect that if necessary, the Lord would raise Isaac from the dead in order to fulfill His covenant regarding that son of promise. (Hebrew 11:19) As it turned out, the Almighty was only testing Abram, and instead of requiring the death of Isaac, at the last moment He stopped Abram from killing his son, and provided a ram as a sacrifice instead.

Yet for all his incredible acts of faith and courage, Abram, like all human beings before and after him (except Jesus Christ), was flawed because of the curse. Not just once, but *twice* he acted cowardly in placing his wife, Sarai in adulterous situations. According to the Bible Sarai was a very beautiful and desirable woman. Upon arriving in Egypt (the breadbasket of the ancient world) during a time of famine in the land of Canaan, Abram told Sarai to deceive the Egyptians by telling them she was Abram's sister rather than his wife. Why? Because Abram knew that when he saw her, Pharaoh would want her. Then Abram, as her husband, would be murdered. So Sarai did as Abram said, and sure enough, Pharaoh took her into his harem. Only after Pharaoh and his household were afflicted with serious diseases because of the imminent sin of adultery, did Abram's deception come to light. In anger, Pharaoh returned his wife to him and sent Abram packing!

Many years later Abraham (his name had been changed by then) stayed in a place named Gerar for a while and did essentially the same thing. This time *he* told them Sarah (her name had also been changed by then) was his sister. Abimelech, king of Gerar then took her for himself. God spoke to the king in a dream one night and told him he was "as good as dead" (Genesis 20:3) for taking a married woman. Yet the Lord in mercy went on to explain to Abimelech that He knew the king had done this innocently, and that He Himself had kept Abimelech from touching Sarah. God assured the king that if he would promptly return her to Abraham, he would be spared. Wisely, Abimelech did just that! Where was the bravery of "the man of faith" on these occasions?

And speaking of "faith," where was Abram's faith when he tried to give God a helping hand in producing the son the Lord had promised him? You can find the sad story of his equivocal behavior in this matter in Genesis chapter 16. In the previous chapter God had promised to give Abram innumerable descendents. It's not clear how much time had passed before the events of chapter 16, when Abram and Sarai took matters into their own hands. But it clearly was enough time for them to have entertained plenty of doubts about how God could fulfill His promise.

Sarai broached the subject. Stating "the LORD has kept me from having children," (Genesis 16:2) she suggested they turn to the customary alternative practiced in their native land. As a barren woman, she offered her handmaiden, an Egyptian named Hagar, to her husband. Hagar would conceive and bear children for Sarai. They soon learned the hard way that *man's customs* are often not *God's way* of doing business. The resulting birth of Ishmael eventually brought heartache and trouble to everyone involved. And it was all because, in this case, "the man of faith" and his wife would not trust God to do what he had promised.

Because of his usual faithfulness, and in spite of his flaws, God loved Abram. Like Noah before him, he truly was a beneficiary of God's grace. In Genesis chapter 15 we read how the Lord had established one of the Scripture's most celebrated covenants with Abram. He began by assuaging Abram's fears and telling him "I am your shield, your very great reward." (Genesis 15:1) Abram responded by asking God what He could possibly give Abram, since he was childless. In those days, a man without children was considered a tragic figure.

God answered him in a classic example of a covenant ceremony. In the events which followed, blood was shed as animals were sacrificed, and the Creator unilaterally committed Himself to Abram and his descendents. The quintessential scene in this narrative occurred when the Lord took Abram outside, and said: "Look up at the heavens and count the stars -- if indeed you can count them... So shall your offspring be." (Genesis 15:5) In the very next verse we learn: "Abram believed the LORD, and God credited it to him as righteousness." (Genesis 15:6) This is the very first explicitly recorded incidence in the Bible of a divine principle which would for the ages to come be referred to as: "righteousness by faith."

God would confirm this covenant with him many years later when Abram was 99 years old. You'll find the details in Genesis chapter 17. In this episode, the Lord changed Abram and Sarai's names and instituted a unique physical sign of the covenant. He also specified the land of Canaan as an *everlasting* possession to Abram and his descendents, and stipulated that *not* Ishmael, but a son as yet unborn would be heir to the promises of the Abrahamic covenant. The birth of that child would be the outcome of a miracle God had planned from the beginning. Abram would be a father again, and Sarai, around the age of 90, would become pregnant with that child.

In conjunction with these predictions, this blessed couple would receive the aforementioned name changes. Abram meant "exalted father." His name would henceforth be Abraham: "father of multitudes." The same Hebrew letter (pronounced "h") which was added to Abram's name was added to his wife's name. Sarai means "my princess." Sarah means "a princess," implying wider recognition as a princess to multitudes. This also signified that she was now royalty not just in her husband's eyes, but in God's eyes, and from her womb divine royalty would ultimately come forth. It anticipated the One who would, in an epoch yet to come, be known as the "Prince of Peace" and the "King of Kings:" Jesus Christ.

What seems to be a rather curious covenant requirement was initiated at this juncture. Every male member of Abraham's household, and every male descendent of his, was to be circumcised. This ritual itself was physical, and as it turns out, its institution demonstrated the wisdom of the Creator of our bodies. Some medical studies have shown a health benefit to both husband and wife from male surgical circumcision. God's wisdom is even evidenced by the timing established for the procedure. Abraham was instructed by God to perform the ritual 8 days after the birth of male children. As it turns out, this is the optimum day for blood coagulation for newborns. In other words, this was the best day for minimizing surgical bleeding. But the real significance of circumcision is not to be found in the physical realm.

Of much greater magnitude was the spiritual symbolism of circumcision. Here again is the shedding of blood as an integral part of the covenant process. There is no escaping the emphasis God consistently places on the giving of blood signifying the giving of life. His covenant people were to give their lives to Him unreservedly. The Abrahamic Covenant was in every respect a blood covenant.

Circumcision involved the removal of *flesh*. Here too is spiritual symbolism. *Flesh* in the Scriptures is representative of human nature corrupted by the curse. Thus the removal of the foreskin from the male sexual organ may depict God's ultimate desire that *spiritually* His children conceive and give birth to *spiritual* descendents not corrupted by the old *fleshly* nature. This would point to the "new covenant" which I'll describe in the next chapter.

A yet further implication of *physical* circumcision, is

that of a circumcision of the human *heart*, or *spirit*. In Deuteronomy 10:15,16 we're presented with this insight: "Yet the LORD set his affection on your forefathers and loved them, and he chose you, their descendents, above all nations, as it is today. Circumcise your *hearts*, therefore..." This allusion is confirmed in the New Testament in Romans 2:28,29: "A man is not a Jew if he is only one outwardly, nor is circumcision merely outward and physical. No, a man is a Jew if he is one inwardly; and circumcision is circumcision of the heart, by the Spirit, not by the written code."

In Acts 7:8 the Abrahamic covenant is actually called "the covenant of circumcision." I believe God chose the token of circumcision because the male foreskin is a layer of flesh which in a sense stands in the way of uninhibited physical intimacy between a man and his wife. In that regard it symbolizes the sin-cursed human nature that hinders spiritual intimacy between man and his God. The kind of covenant the Lord desires with humanity is one of a loving heart relationship, unhindered by any flesh. Perhaps more than anything, the Abrahamic Covenant represents God's inherent desire to love and fellowship deeply with men and women.

This covenant was again reinforced in the wake of Abraham's astounding act of faith and obedience in his willingness to sacrificially offer his son of promise, Isaac, to the Lord. I cited this event previously. Immediately following it, a *general* promise was distilled into a *particular* promise, as we'll see in a moment. The saga is recounted in Genesis chapter 22. The narrative of Abraham's willingness to sacrifice his son is one of the most moving stories in all of history. It's an awesome thing for a person to sacrifice their own life. But it is nothing short of staggering to think of a loving parent sacrificing their own child. Abraham's willingness to give his son's life prefigures the future death of the Heavenly Father's Son. I'll not take the space here to itemize them, but the parallels between the two events are striking.

God's great heart was deeply stirred by the love and loyalty Abraham had demonstrated to Him in that moment. He reiterated His pledge to give Abraham innumerable descendents, and in Genesis 22:18 added: "...and through *your offspring* all nations on earth will be blessed..." The Hebrew word for offspring is in the *singular* form here, and literally means "seed." While this passage looks forward in time, it also looks back to the very first promise of a coming Redeemer. It's a reference to the offspring (or seed) of the woman, first mentioned in Genesis 3:15, who would someday overcome sin, Satan, and the curse on behalf of all mankind. Further, the connection of these two biblical accounts reminds us that the ultimate promised divine offspring would trace his ancestry through both men and women.

In the New Testament the Apostle Paul further enlightens us as to the significance of this word to Abraham. "The promises were spoken to Abraham and to his seed. The Scripture does not say 'and to seeds,' meaning many people, but 'and to your seed,' meaning one person, who is Christ." (Galatians 3:16) *Christ* is the Greek word closest in equivalence to the Hebrew word *Messiah*, a title meaning "anointed one." This title was first applied to the future *offspring of Abraham* in the book of the prophet Daniel. (Daniel 9:25,26) God had extended the honor of being the forefather of the Messiah and Redeemer of all humanity to His friend, Abraham!

The Abrahamic Covenant was designed to reestablish an intimate relationship between God and men through Abraham and his descendents, and in due course to conquer the curse and restore the blessing of God to the whole earth. Several centuries later God would establish another covenant with His people, related to the previous one, but distinctly different.

In Genesis 15:13-16 the Lord had told Abram that his descendents would some day be enslaved and mistreated in another country for 400 years, then return to the land God had promised to them. The man God chose to lead them out of that bondage in Egypt was Moses. Born of Jewish parents, but adopted by Pharaoh's daughter and highly trained as a son of privilege in the courts of Egyptian royalty, Moses was being uniquely prepared for his future calling. That preparation would also include his eventual flight from Egypt as a wanted killer, then 40 years working for his father-in-law as a shepherd in the ancient land of Midian. By the time God fully revealed His call to an 80 year old Moses at Mount Horeb, the Almighty's chosen deliverer for Israel was a humbled man. But he was the man for whom the Lord had been looking.

You can read all the particulars of the story of Moses' encounter with the Lord in Exodus chapters 3 and 4. From a burning bush which refused to be consumed, God called out His servant's name: "Moses! Moses!" (Exodus 3:4) The inarticulate shepherd responded simply with a respectful "Here I am." (Exodus 3:4) God warned Moses not to come closer, and commanded him to take off his sandals in deference to the holy ground on which he was standing.

The Lord then identified Himself as the God of Abraham and his descendents. He presented the fearful Moses with his assignment, laying out for him the misery of his people back in Egypt, and revealing His intentions to use Moses to bring them out of slavery into the promised land of Canaan. The Lord had barely finished His discourse when this would-be leader began making excuses. At first God patiently dealt with each of Moses' concerns, lovingly alleviating each anxiety. But when the reluctant leader eventually pleaded for God to "please send someone else to do it," (Exodus 4:13) the Lord's patience had reached its limit. He stooped to Moses' weakness and provided a solution, but not before He expressed His anger at Moses' resistance to God's calling.

What did God see in this reticent runaway? We might discern little in Moses' life at this time to recommend him. But God sees deep inside each heart, and He knows the future as well as the past and present. Moses' previous experience had been a tool in the hand of the Lord, shaping and preparing him for his divine destiny. And impending events would not only continue to cultivate his character, they would expose to generations as yet unborn, the seed of greatness that was already in Moses' heart.

This reluctant leader would become a powerful man of faith. The miracles which occurred on his watch were among the most astounding in history. The ten supernatural plagues wrought by God through Moses brought the idolatrous leader of the world's super power of that era to his knees. The last of those plagues was the death of all the firstborn offspring of men and animals. During that remarkable final night in Egypt, only the firstborn of the Jews were spared by the death angel because of the application of the blood of an innocent lamb to the doorway of each Israeli home. The death angel passed over those dwellings in a supernatural event which is still celebrated by Jews today as the "Passover." This event was a harbinger of the death and resurrection of Jesus.

Having finally been granted freedom for his people by Pharaoh, the following day Moses and the children of Israel set out on their journey to the promised land. Quickly recanting his release of God's people, Pharaoh and his army set out in hot pursuit of his former slaves. He soon appeared to have the Israelites trapped "between the devil and the deep blue sea." But in one unprecedented act of divine deliverance, Moses raised his staff and the Lord separated the waters of the Red Sea to allow the people of Israel to miraculously cross over to freedom on dry ground. Then after the Israelites had reached the other side, by God's power Moses rejoined the waters to drown the mighty Pharaoh and his finest charioteers.

During the trek to the promised land, still more stupendous wonders took place. Water enough to quench the thirst of millions burst forth from solid rock! Day after day, year after year, nutritious heavenly food inexplicably appeared on the ground each morning at sunrise! And when the people got tired of it and complained they wanted meat, a wind delivered enough fowl to allow the folks to stuff themselves sick!

Yet an incident related in Numbers 11:24-30 offers testimony to the fact that Moses was a very modest man. In spite of the astonishing deeds which had made him a virtual superstar, he refused to jealously guard his exclusive status. When the Lord poured His Spirit out on 70 elders of Israel who subsequently prophesied, Moses refused to react by worrying that this public visitation of God upon those 70 elders might result in a challenge to his own authority. Instead, he only wished to see all God's people exercise the same divine power as he had. This *great leader* obviously possessed *great humility.* Numbers 12:3 later confirms: "Now Moses was a very humble man, more humble than anyone else on the face of the earth."

Miracles aside, what pleased the hearts of both God and Moses most was the intimacy between them. Exodus 33:11 describes their encounters thus: "The LORD would speak to Moses face to face, *as a man speaks with his friend."* Psalm 103:7 unveils another glimpse into the nature of their kinship. It says: "He [God]* made known his *ways* to Moses, his *deeds* to the people of Israel..." The masses may on occasions witness the grand exploits of the Almighty, but only the intimate fully understand the character and motivations behind those actions. Moses was always hungry to know the Lord better. In Exodus 33:18 we find him asking God to show him His glory. And the Lord graciously complied with that request because He was pleased with Moses.

I believe that the most telling indication of the closeness of their relationship was revealed when the Lord told Moses that because of a great sin committed by his fellow Jews, God would no longer accompany them on their journey, but would only send His angel before them instead. After God relented in response to the pleas of Moses, and declared His presence would go with the Israelites after all, the man of God cried out: "If your Presence does not go with us, do not send us up from here." (Exodus 33:15)

Those whom God loves most dearly are the ones who treasure His presence above all else. Moses was that kind of person.

Moses' earlier shortcomings were on display in the encounter with God at the burning bush. He had grown much as a man of God since then. But like Abraham before him, Moses was still not perfect. In Numbers chapter 20 we read the story of how, during one of those incidents when God used him to provide water for his constantly murmuring brethren, Moses lost his temper. Instead of simply speaking to the rock as the Lord had clearly commanded him, Moses angrily struck it with his staff. It cost him dearly. God advised Moses that because of this dishonorable behavior, he would not be allowed to enter the promised land with his people. This great but defective man, whose life we've just briefly highlighted for you, was the individual through whom the Lord would present His next major covenant with humans.

God had already established a relationship with the people of Israel through the covenant He had made with their ancestor, Abraham. By means of the Abrahamic Covenant they had become the people of promise. Now God would establish a pact *directly* with them. Exodus chapter 19 ushers in this new contract between the Lord and His special people. 50 days after God had delivered them from Egypt through the original Passover, He began to communicate the covenant to Moses. They were in the wilderness on the way to the land the Lord had promised to them through Abraham. The Israelites were camped at Mount Sinai at the time, and it was on that mountain that God gave them the covenant through Moses. Thus the pact has come to be called the Siniatic Covenant.

Not coincidently, Mount Sinai is another name for Mount Horeb, the very same peak where Moses had earlier encountered the divine presence at the burning bush.

Before this covenant was delivered, God reminded the Jews of His loving care for them and His plans for them to become a unique witness to the rest of the world. "You yourselves have seen what I did to Egypt, and how I carried you on eagle's wings and brought you to myself. Now if you obey me fully and keep my covenant, then out of all nations you will be my treasured possession. Although the whole earth is mine, you will be for me a kingdom of priests and a holy nation." (Exodus 19:4-6)

The elders (leaders) of Israel responded: "We will do everything the LORD has said." (Exodus 19:8) So God had Moses give clear-cut instructions to prepare the people to receive the covenant 3 days later. When the third day arrived, thunder, lightning, and a thick cloud emerged on Mount Sinai, and a very loud trumpet sounded. The Lord descended onto the mountain in fire and smoke and the whole towering mass trembled. The trumpet blast grew stronger and stronger until God called Moses up to meet Him on the top of the mountain. There the Lord gave him, on tablets of stone in God's own writing, the essence of the covenant: the Ten Commandments. This "Decalogue" comprised the *moral laws* at the heart of the Siniatic Covenant. They would be followed by two additional categories: the *civil laws* and the *ceremonial* (or worship) *laws.* Altogether, the verbalization of these various laws consumes the bulk of the next dozen chapters in the book of Exodus.

Why did God move from a relatively brief and simple covenant agreement with Abraham, to a quite lengthy and detailed one with the nation descended from him? From one standpoint we can all recognize that dealing with an individual is quite different from dealing with a whole nation. Many centuries of history had demonstrated that relatively few individuals were as willing as Noah, Abraham, and Moses to develop a close working relationship with the Lord. How would God communicate His heart and mind to a group of people who would not intimately commune with Him, and therefore be unable to hear His voice clearly and definitively on these matters? To bring an entire populace in line with the will of the Almighty would require an extensive written codification of His principles for living. The laws of the Siniatic Covenant were just that.

But God had more than practical sociology in mind when He established the law. There was a deeply spiritual purpose, too. What was that purpose? The answer may shock you. "The law was added so that the trespass [sin]* might increase." If this bold and unexpected assertion found in Romans 5:20 initially confuses us, the Apostle Paul's claim two chapters later may stand us on our heads! "For I would not have known what coveting really was if the law had not said, 'Do not covet.' But sin, seizing the opportunity afforded by the commandment, produced in me every kind of covetous desire. For apart from the law sin is dead." (Romans 7:7,8)

Why in the world would the Lord want sin to increase? It is not simply the *act of sin* which increased because of the introduction of the law, but *awareness of sin*. Romans 3:20 clarifies this principle: "...through the law we become *conscious* of sin." The popular conception that the law of God was given through Moses to make people behave righteously is erroneous. No law of any kind can make a person *do* what is right. It can only *show us* what is right and what is wrong. The consequences of breaking the law may help motivate us to do right, but neither the law nor its consequences can *compel* us to behave accordingly. Parents need only to look at the strong-willed child who defiantly does exactly what they tell him *not to do,* to realize this fact of fallen human nature.

So it is with the law of God. Romans 3:20 clearly states: "...*no one* will be declared righteous in his [God's]* sight by observing the law..." Why? A few verses later in Romans 3:23, the Apostle Paul declares: "...for all have sinned and fallen short..." No one (except Jesus Christ) has ever or will ever be able to perfectly keep the law of God. And if you can't keep the *entire* law you cannot be declared righteous through that law. The Apostle James is unequivocal on this matter: "For whoever keeps the whole law and yet stumbles at one point is guilty of breaking all of it." (James 2:10) The law was not given to make us righteous, it was given to convince us of our utter moral and spiritual bankruptcy. The curse has so affected and afflicted us that we fallen humans are totally incapable of ever being right with God on our own!

The book of Galatians represents the law as something of a legal guardian over God's children, until they reach a certain level of maturity. It further explains that this guardianship was preparing them for something fuller and better. "So the law was put in charge to lead us to Christ..." (Galatians 3:24) The Greek word here translated "put in charge" is a compound one, taken from the word for "boy, or child" and the word for "to lead." It literally means a "boy-leader." The law was intended to supervise the children of God for the purpose of leading them to the Christ, or Messiah, the offspring (seed) of Abraham, through whom not only Israel, but *all nations* on earth were to be blessed. After that, it's work was finished. The law was not an end in itself, but an interim guardian.

The law extends before us an unreachable carrot of blessings, while brandishing an inescapable stick of curses. Interestingly, Strong's Concordance gives the definition of the Greek word for "boy" cited in the previous paragraph as: "a boy (*as often beaten with impunity*)." The first 14 verses of Deuteronomy chapter 28 list the blessings to be enjoyed by God's people who "fully obey the Lord" and "carefully follow all his commands." (Deuteronomy 28:1) The last 54 verses inventory the curses which will fall on those who "do not carefully follow all his commands and decrees." (Deuteronomy 28:15) The history of the nation of Israel illustrates the end result of human efforts to obtain the blessings in our own strength. They experienced those blessings only in limited fashion. And that was more due to the mercy and grace of the Lord than their own achievements. But they suffered under a heavy measure of the curses that come from rebellion against God's commands. Theirs is the destiny of all who attempt to obtain the blessings of God through their own good works. We always fall short and finish up under the curse instead. The failure is not with the law of God... it is with us!

Still, the law did not leave us in complete despair. As stated previously, it was a guardian responsible for leading God's people to their ultimate Savior. As such it offered a *provisional* way out, which foreshadowed an *eternal* solution. Under its ceremonial laws, it provided for the sacrificial death of an animal to atone (make amends) for sins and acquire acceptability before God. This practice would reconcile sinners to a holy Lord, restoring their relationship with Him. Bulls, goats, rams, and lambs died in place of people, giving their lifeblood on behalf of sin-cursed human beings.

Animal sacrifice had been an aspect of mankind's relationship with their Maker ever since the fall in the Garden of Eden. You may remember that the first animal sacrifice was performed by God Himself, as He slew animals in order to use their skins to cover the nakedness of Adam and Eve. The death of the animals was not actually mentioned in the biblical context of that event... it was simply implied.

Other sacrifices would follow in the unfolding stories of the Scriptures. Abel offered sacrifices to the Lord from his flocks. With the post-flood burnt offerings of Noah we again see men have a hand in these sacrifices. Gradually more understanding of the significance of this ceremony would be afforded to humans. When Abram obeyed God's instructions by sacrificing animals at the establishment of the Lord's covenant with him, we discover God and man cooperating in the ceremony, and sense a connection between sacrifice and the covenant relationship of God to man. In the original Passover (Exodus chapters 11 and 12) we observe the *substitutionary* nature of animal sacrifice.

Now in the law, still further comprehension of the objective of animal sacrifice was afforded. Essentially, two types of sacrifices (or offerings) were described: voluntary ones for expressing worship to the Lord, and mandatory ones to deal with sin. There were various sin and guilt offerings for priests, leaders, individuals, and the whole community or nation. These were all intended to atone for sin, and through them God plainly shows us that animal sacrifice under the Siniatic Covenant was an answer to the sin problem and its attendant curse.

The most notable of the sin offerings is described in Leviticus chapter 16, and took place on the annual Day of Atonement, or as it is known in Hebrew: Yom Kippur. On that occasion two goats were to be used. One shed its blood in atonement for the all the sins of Israel committed during the past year. The other was called the "scapegoat." (Leviticus 16:11) After the high priest laid his hands on its head and confessed all the wickedness, rebellion, and sins of the nation over it, this goat was driven out into the wilderness, carrying with it all the sins of the people. Increasingly, animal sacrifices pointed to one ultimate sacrifice yet to come, preparing our understanding for it.

While the Siniatic Covenant *succeeded* the Abrahamic Covenant, it did not *replace* it. In making the case that the Seed of Abraham (Jesus Christ) brings us the promised blessings of the Abrahamic Covenant rather than the curses of the law of the Siniatic Covenant, the Apostle Paul stressed the superiority of the former. In Galatians 3:17 he says: "What I mean is this: The law, introduced 430 years later, does not set aside the covenant previously established by God and thus do away with the promise." The coming Messiah was to be a fulfillment of the promise of God to Abraham to bless all nations through his offspring. In so doing, this Savior would redeem us from the curses of sin and the law, and establish a *new* covenant... a true covenant of the *heart*

*Not in the original text. Added by the author for clarification.

CHAPTER 7

The Promised Offspring

Stand with me at the back of a courtroom. Before us is a crowd gathered to witness crucial legal proceedings about to be consummated. At the focal point a compassionate, yet sober-faced magistrate, draped in his impeccable judicial robe, peers over the bench at a member of a notorious crime family who has been found guilty of capital offenses. Now with heart pounding and head swimming, the once arrogant criminal anxiously awaits his sentence. He knows his very life is at stake. Slowly, deliberately, the judge begins to speak. "You have been convicted of terrible deeds. The law leaves me no choice as to your fate. In due punishment for your crimes I sentence you to death!"

A swarm of loud voices erupts. Some cheer the sentence and jeer the condemned man. Others weep, begging in vain for mercy for the man whose head hangs low in doomed despair. Before the clamor fades, we hear the doors just behind us suddenly swing open, and a man with purposeful stride brushes past us, moving quickly toward the bench. The parting crowd hardly has time to consider who this interloper is or why he has come, when he lifts his head and voice to resolutely address the judge. "Your honor, I wish to take the place of this condemned man. I will be his substitute. I will die for his crimes."

The once boisterous assembly is now hushed into stunned silence. No one in the throng had anticipated such an event. The judge seems moved by this sacrificial proposition. Every bit as engrossed as the astonished crowd at the front of the courtroom, you and I await his reaction. The judge leans forward and looks carefully into the face of the would-be redeemer. He soon clearly recognizes the man. With focused mind and steadfast authority he responds. The judge's revelation brings this whole intriguing episode to a startling conclusion. "No sir, you may *not* die for this man! For you are a fugitive from justice yourself... a member of this same family of criminals. You must die for *your own* crimes. You cannot take the place of your brother!" As police arrest and remove the unsuccessful savior and his condemned brother to lock-up, we're all left to ponder the implications of this extraordinary scene.

The above fictional account is intended to lay a foundation for our understanding of the most pivotal event in the history of the world. The one who was to be the Christ, Messiah, Savior, Redeemer of humanity could not possibly be a fellow sinner. He had to be unique. He must be one of us... yet He must *not* be one of us! He must be fully human, but without the old sinful nature passed along genetically to all other human beings. He must also be without a single sinful act of His own. Who could possibly fulfill these seemingly impossible qualifications? The answer to this question had been determined even before the initial moment in time when the need for a redeemer had arisen. We read in I Peter 1:18-20: "For you know that it was not with silver or gold that you were redeemed from the empty way of life handed down to you from your forefathers, but with the precious blood of Christ, a lamb without blemish or defect. He was chosen *before the creation of the world*, but was revealed in these last times for your sake."

The statement "He was chosen *before the creation of the world…*" confronts us with one of the most difficult concepts surrounding divinity: that of eternity. God is eternal. He had no beginning and will have no end. He has always been, and always will be. On the other hand, we have been creatures of time; living since our inception in a realm defined by seconds, minutes, hours, days, weeks, months, years, centuries, and millennia. We do have an understanding of this thing called *time*. *Eternity*, on the other hand, tends to elude our full intellectual grasp… particularly the notion of something or someone that *has always been*.

It's very difficult for us to look back through time and envision such a thing. Our lives have been replete with beginnings, and it's nearly incomprehensible to imagine someone or something that never had a moment of origin. At least we're inclined to possess an innate sense of life with no end. Although we intellectually know that every person will die someday, there is somehow within each of us an indefinable feeling that we were designed to live forever. I'm convinced that this spark of awareness of eternity emerges irrepressibly from the fact that we were created by God to possess life without end. Ecclesiastes 3:11 suggests that this concept is an implant from the Lord

Himself. "He has made everything beautiful in its time. He has also set eternity in the hearts of men; yet they cannot fathom what God has done from beginning to end."

While the above passage clearly indicates that the notion of eternity is in our hearts, the latter part of that verse seems to allude to the limitations of our understanding of that divine notion. At some level we can usually conceive of life with _no end_... but _no beginning_? Any attempt to comprehend an entity with no beginning can boggle our time-constricted minds.

That the Lord dwells in eternity means He is not confined by the limits of time. He sees the _beginning_ and _end_ of time... plus everything before, after, and in between! He knew before He created man, that this creature whom He had lovingly formed in His own image, would fall into sin and rebel against His benevolent rule. So the plan to redeem people from sin and its curse was prepared before the actual event ever occurred in the realm of time. Nothing takes God by surprise. He anticipated the fall of man, and He knew who and what it would take to restore man from the degradation of sin back into blessed fellowship with Himself.

Jesus of Nazareth was unique in all history. He was born into the _sinful_ race of man, yet was born _sinless,_ and remained so to His last breath. He was fully God and fully human. The unique circumstances of His birth made this all possible. As foretold in the very first prophecy of the coming Redeemer (Genesis 3:15), Jesus was the offspring of woman. And in fulfillment of the prediction made centuries earlier in Isaiah 7:14, that woman was a virgin. Matthew 1:18 documents the fulfillment: "This is how the birth of Jesus Christ came about: His mother

Mary was pledged to be married to Joseph, but before they came together, she was found to be with child through the Holy Spirit." In some undefined manner, the Holy Spirit of God came down from heaven to impregnate a woman on earth. So Jesus was the consummation of human ovum *and* divine insemination.

He went on to live a sinless life, thus He had no sin of His own for which to pay a penalty. His humanity authorized Him to be the substitute for the entire race in paying the penalty for *our* sins. Jesus was born in innocence as was Adam. And Jesus was tempted by the devil like Adam. But unlike Adam, Jesus never sinned. Jesus was and is the only one ever qualified to be the Savior of the world.

His unparalleled pedigree had still another repercussion. Jesus became in effect the *last* of the old line of human beings and the *first* of a new one. In I Corinthians 15:45-49 the Apostle Paul explains: "So it is written: 'The first Adam became a living being,' the last Adam [Jesus]*, a life-giving spirit. The spiritual did not come first, but the natural, and after that the spiritual. The first man was of the dust of the earth, the second man from heaven. As was the earthly man, so are those who are of the earth; and as is the man from heaven, so also are those who are of heaven. And just as we have born the likeness of the earthly man, so shall we bear the likeness of the man from heaven."

In His humanity, Jesus was the last of Adam's descendents. But additionally, He was and is the first of a very different kind of man. Just how radically improved the spiritual heritage of this new kind of man was to be, is illustrated by a comment Jesus made concerning John the Baptist in Luke 7:28: "I tell you, among those born of women there is no one greater than John; yet the one who is least in the kingdom of God is greater than he." In other words, the *least* of this new order of human beings "born again" through Christ is superior to the *greatest* of the old order descended from Adam.

Romans 8:29 tells us that those who would put their faith in Jesus Christ were destined by God "...to be conformed to the likeness of his Son [Jesus]*, that he might be the first-born among many brothers." Romans 8:17 further says: "Now if we are [God's]* children, then we are heirs -- heirs of God and co-heirs with Christ..." The *first Adam's* descendents traced their ancestry from *Adam* through all succeeding generations of forefathers. Those of the *last Adam* (Jesus) are in the spiritual sense not so much His *descendents*, but His *brothers*, and co-heirs of God with Him. Through the *first Adam* we have many fathers, beginning with *Adam*. Through the *last Adam* (Jesus) we are the direct children of *God* Himself. That's why Jesus instructed His disciples: "And do not call anyone on earth 'father,' for you have one Father, and he is in heaven." (Matthew 23:9)

Jesus constantly spoke of God as *His* Father, and the Father *of all who followed Jesus*. He taught His disciples to begin their prayers by addressing God as "Our Father." (Matthew 6:9) This was a revolutionary concept for that era. The Old Testament rarely referred to God as Father. In fact, it was because of His claim that God was His Father that the Pharisees (a powerful sect of Judaism at the time of Jesus) accused Him of blasphemy and sought to kill Him. In Mark 14:36 we find the Lord Jesus, just hours from His death, agonizing in prayer in anticipation of the awful suffering He was about to endure. Here He addressed God as "Abba, Father."

"Abba" is neither Greek nor English, but a literal rendering of an Aramaic word. Linguist W.E. Vine explains that "Abba" was used by infants, and represents an attitude of unreasoning trust. The Greek word translated "Father" in this passage expresses an intelligent apprehension of the relationship of father and child. Used together as Jesus did here, these two words represent both the simple innocent love of a child, *and* the mature intelligent confidence of an adult. The use of this trustful, endearing, and intimate term "Abba," was not just for Jesus, but its legitimate use is through Him extended to every true believer, as we're told in Romans 8:15 and Galatians 4:6. The nearest modern English equivalents to "Abba" might be "daddy" or "papa." Through our Savior, we who have been born again have become the trusting children of our loving "Heavenly Daddy."

Jesus of Nazareth was the promised seed, or offspring, of Abraham. For many centuries the Jewish people were fastidious about recording their genealogies. There were a number of reasons for this. Since the root through which the blessing of God flowed to them was Abraham, it was vital to verify that link to him. Specific promises had been given to each tribe (family branch descended from each of their forefathers - Jacob's 12 sons) within the nation, and the genealogies documented their tribal identification. This was particularly important for the tribe of Levi, from whom exclusively came the priesthood. God-ordained royalty was to descend from the line of the godly King David, who was of the tribe of Judah. These were among the reasons why the Israelites were so devoted to maintaining accurate genealogic documents. But of paramount importance was the anticipation of validating the arrival of the promised offspring of Abraham: the Messiah, or Christ, through whom not only Israel, but *all* nations of the earth would be blessed.

Two of the four gospels of the New Testament (Matthew and Luke) include a genealogy tracing the human ancestry of Jesus. Matthew actually begins his account of the life of Christ with this genealogy, documenting the lineage from Abraham through Joseph, Jesus' adoptive father. Technically, this was not required since Jesus was conceived of the Holy Spirit and born of the virgin Mary, and thus He was not a biological descendent of Joseph. Still, it reinforces the legitimacy of Jesus' claim to be the Promised One. Luke, on the other hand, introduces his genealogy later, in chapter 3, outlining Jesus' ancestors all the way back to Adam. He traces this lineage through the males in the ancestry of Jesus' biological mother, Mary. Both genealogies also demonstrate that Jesus was not only the offspring of Abraham, but furthermore, of the royal line of King David, through whom also it was promised that the Messiah would come.

But it was not these genealogies alone which proved that Jesus of Nazareth was the promised Redeemer. There were many other confirmations. Let's look first at the prophecies which Jesus of Nazareth fulfilled concerning various aspects of the coming of the Christ. There are more than 300 predictions in the Old Testament regarding the Messiah. Many of them were made thousands of years before the time of Christ. They range from forecasts of His virgin birth in Bethlehem to details of the cruel death He would die as a sacrifice for the sins of the world. Statisticians have calculated the odds of one man completely fulfilling every detail of each of these hundreds of prophecies. The resulting probability ratio is so staggeringly minute as to set the chances of a single individual satisfying all these predictions at virtually *zero*. In other words, just based upon His fulfillment of these prophecies, Jesus *had to be* the Promised One. Yet there were more signs.

His words possessed a power never before experienced by those who first heard Him. As a 12 year old boy Jesus astounded adults with His knowledge. While with His parents in Jerusalem for the annual Passover Feast, He conversed at length with the teachers in the temple courts. His spiritual understanding and answers to their questions amazed everyone. (Luke 2:47) His first public speaking as an adult stunned His neighbors. After reading at the synagogue from a prophecy of the Messiah in the book of Isaiah, He sat down, and every eye was magnetically drawn to Him. He then affirmed to them that He was the Messiah, saying: "Today this scripture is fulfilled in your hearing." (Luke 4:21) They were flabbergasted at His gracious words, wondering how such eloquence could flow from the son of Joseph, a mere carpenter. At His initial out of town public appearance, in the Galilean village of Capernaum, "They were amazed at his teaching, because his message had authority." (Luke 4:32)

Nearly everywhere He ventured, Jesus healed incurable diseases, cast out evil spirits, and commanded nature itself to obey Him. He performed miracles at such a prodigious rate that in alluding to His many deeds, the Apostle John mused at the close of his gospel: "If every one of them were written down, I suppose that even the whole world would not have room for the books that would be written." (John 21:25)

The respected Pharisee, Nicodemus, came to Jesus one night and confessed: "...we know you are a teacher who has come from God. For no one could perform the miraculous signs you are doing if God were not with him." (John 3:2) When at the Feast of Dedication at Jerusalem they pressed Him to tell them plainly if He were actually the Christ. He directed them to His demonstration of supernatural power: "The miracles I do in my Father's name speak for me..." (John 10:25) And when his own cousin, John the Baptist, while languishing in a dungeon for preaching righteousness, expressed momentary doubts as to Jesus' true identity, Jesus told John's disciples: "Go back and report to John what you hear and see: The blind receive sight, the lame walk, those who have leprosy are cured, the deaf hear, the dead are raised, and the good news is preached to the poor." (Matthew 11:4,5)

Every aspect of Jesus' life exuded the holiness and love of God the Father. His behavior was righteous, and His teachings were righteous, because His heart was righteous... set apart unto God, His Father. He spent long periods alone, seeking the face of God in prayer, and came away from those times of communion knowing just what was the right thing to do in every situation, and having the power to do it. In John 8:29 Jesus professed: "The one who has sent me [God the Father]* is with me; he has not left me alone, for I always do what pleases him."

Whenever He encountered things which were not right, He did what He could to set them right. Yet in all His zeal for absolute holiness, He looked past human sin and frailty into hearts hungry for God, and loved them deeply.

He even taught His disciples: "Love your enemies, do good to those who hate you, bless those who curse you, pray for those who mistreat you." (Luke 6:27,28) And He practiced what He preached. When Judas Iscariot came that awful night to betray him, Jesus, knowing exactly what Judas was up to, greeted him as "friend." (Matthew 26:50) And while dying in unthinkable agony, He lifted His great heart to His Heavenly Father and asked for forgiveness for those sinners who perpetrated the terrible deed. Jesus taught us that divine holiness and divine love are not mutually exclusive. And in so doing He revealed the character of the Father with whom He shared divinity.

But there was no greater proof of Jesus' messiahship and divinity than His death and resurrection. Strange and awesome goings-on took place while a sinless Jesus, the very Son of God, hung on a cross outside Jerusalem dying for the sins of every person who had ever lived and would ever live. From noon until 3:00 PM a peculiar darkness fell over the whole land. Back in the city, at the exact moment of His death, the massive, heavy curtain of the temple was mysteriously torn in two from top to bottom. The earth trembled, ancient tombs of long departed righteous people broke open, and many of these folks rose from the dead and were seen by significant numbers of the city's population. Back at the site of the cross, the Roman centurion on duty exclaimed: "Surely he was the Son of God!" (Matthew 27:54) It was through Jesus' crucifixion that the way was opened for restoration of the relationship with God which had been lost by disobedience in the Garden of Eden. Paul explained to the church at Corinth: "...God was reconciling the world to himself in Christ, not counting men's sins against them." (II Corinthians 5:19)

If His death plainly bore witness to His identity as the Savior of the world, His resurrection from that death effectively thundered its declaration of that identity: **This is the Promised One of God! No grave can hold Him!** The fact that He rose from the dead is what makes Jesus Christ distinct from all other religious figures in history. As the Apostle Paul asserts in Romans 1:4, He "...was declared with power to be the Son of God by His resurrection from the dead: Jesus Christ our Lord."

And no other ancient event is so thoroughly authenticated and well-documented as the resurrection of Jesus. There were over 500 witnesses of the risen Christ. (I Corinthians 15:6) All 4 Gospels record the details of the resurrection, and numerous other books of the New Testament make extensive reference to it. These books were all written within a half century of the resurrection, so if it were untrue, the authors' assertions concerning it would have been easily refuted by surviving eyewitnesses. And it should be noted that there are far more early manuscripts of the books of the New Testament than of any other ancient historical documents.

These events in the life and ministry of Jesus Christ ushered in the New Covenant spoken of by the Old Testament man of God known as the "weeping prophet." The details are to be found in Jeremiah chapter 31.There, when through the culmination of its habitual rebellion and idolatry, Israel had finally alienated itself from their God, the weeping prophet wiped his eyes and cleared his vision enough to see a brighter day ahead. "'The time is coming,' declares the LORD, 'when I will make a new covenant with the house of Israel... It will not be like the covenant I made with their forefathers when I took them by the hand to lead them out of Egypt, because they broke my covenant, though I was a husband to them,' declares the LORD. 'This is the covenant I will make with the house of Israel after that time,' declares the LORD. 'I will put my law in their minds and write it on their hearts. I will be their God and they will be my people. No longer will a man teach his neighbor, or a man his brother, saying, Know the LORD, because they will all know me, from the least of them to the greatest,' declares the LORD. 'For I will forgive their wickedness and will remember their sins no more.'" (Jeremiah 31:31-34) This New Covenant would replace the Old (or Siniatic) Covenant.

That's not to say there was a defect in the law of the Old Covenant. Jesus Himself addressed that issue when He said in Matthew 5:17: "Do not think that I have come to abolish the Law or the Prophets; I have not come to abolish them but to fulfill them." The problem was with the *people* of the Old Covenant... and for that matter, all the people of earth. Try though we might, in our fallen state we are incapable of fully keeping the law. Only Jesus was able to do that. However; even while He fulfilled the Old Testament law, He was instituting a higher, simpler law, and a new way of living. The Apostle John defines this new way of life as follows: "For the law was given through Moses; grace and truth came through Jesus Christ." (John 1:17)

In Matthew 22:37-40 we discover Jesus teaching men a higher, yet simpler law. He referred them back to a passage from Deuteronomy 6:5: "'Love the LORD your God with all your heart and with all your soul and with all your mind.' This is the first and greatest commandment." Then quoting from Leviticus 19:18, He went on: "And the second is like it: 'Love your neighbor as yourself.' All the Law and the Prophets hang on these two commandments." Paul summed it up this way: "…love is the fulfillment of the law." (Romans 13:10) The life Jesus lived exemplified love toward God in His constant intimate communion with, and His total faith in and obedience to, His Heavenly Father. And through His love for His neighbor (that is, His fellowmen) He became the perfect example of His own axiom that "Greater love has no one than this, that he lay down his life for his friends." (John 15:13) It was through that redemptive death that He established the New Covenant.

The Lord Jesus first announced the New Covenant to His disciples the night before His death, as He celebrated the annual Passover meal with them. Mark 14:22-24 records the event as follows: "While they were eating, Jesus took bread, gave thanks and broke it, and gave it to his disciples, saying, 'Take it; this is my body.' Then He took the cup, gave thanks and offered it to them, and they all drank from it. 'This is my blood of the covenant, which is poured out for many,' he said to them."

His companions would have been familiar with the sacrificial Passover lamb, whose flesh and blood delivered their ancestors from death during the last plague which fell upon the Egyptians before the Jews were delivered from bondage. Yet they would not immediately recognize that Jesus' impending death was about to make Him the sacrificial lamb of a fresh pact with God. Jesus was soon to become, as John the Baptist had proclaimed of Him three and a half years earlier: "…the Lamb of God, who takes away the sin of the world!" (John 1:29)

The death of Jesus paralleled not only that of the original

Passover lamb, but that of all the bulls, rams, lambs, and goats slaughtered by the priests for the sins of the people of Israel, under the laws of the Old Covenant. Those animal sacrifices were only symbolic short-term measures, anticipating God's ultimate provision for atonement of sin and reconciliation of mankind with Himself. Hebrews 10:3,4 expresses the inadequacy of animal offerings, stating: "But those sacrifices are an annual reminder of sins, because it is impossible for the blood of bulls and goats to take away sins." That Jesus' crucifixion was the final solution to the sin problem is confirmed in Hebrews 7:27. "Unlike the other high priests, he [Jesus]* does not need to offer sacrifices day after day, first for his own sins, and then for the sins of the people. He sacrificed for their sins once for all when he offered himself."

The Promised One, through whom all nations of the earth would be *blessed*, Himself became a *curse*, in order to deliver from the *curse* of the Old Covenant all who would put their faith in Him. He could do this because He was the only human being who ever completely fulfilled the law, and therefore He could bear the curse due upon the rest of us who have all fallen short. "Christ redeemed us from the curse of the law by becoming a curse for us, for it is written: 'Cursed is everyone who is hung on a tree.' He redeemed us in order that the blessing given to Abraham might also come to the Gentiles [non-Jews]* through Christ Jesus, so that by faith we might receive the promise of the Spirit." (Galatians 3:13,14) It is this promise of the Holy Spirit, who comes to live in the hearts of all true believers in Jesus, which enables us to have the law of God written in our *hearts and minds* under the New Covenant. As we noted a few paragraphs earlier, the Lord had pledged this inner transformation centuries before through the prophet Jeremiah.

Notice also that Galatians 3:14 indicates that the sacrificial death of Jesus Christ restores and expands the reach of the blessing of the Abrahamic Covenant. Remember, that covenant was one of the "heart," as declared in Romans 2:29, which we cited in the previous chapter. Through the New Covenant in the blood of Jesus, God was moving us back toward the intimate heart fellowship with Him that He had intended from the very beginning. The New Covenant reverts past the *works* (deeds) based righteousness of the law of the Siniatic Covenant, to the *faith* based righteousness of the Abrahamic Covenant.

In Galatians 3:6,7 the Apostle Paul says: "Consider Abraham: 'He believed God, and it was credited to him as righteousness.' Understand then, that those who believe are children of Abraham." In one sense the New Covenant restores the Abrahamic Covenant. But in another sense it supersedes it, since the Abrahamic Covenant could only *look forward* to the coming Messiah and the divine reconciliation provided by His death and resurrection. The New Covenant *looks back* on those events as accomplished facts, and opens the blessing of Abraham to the whole population of planet earth, not just to the *physical descendents* of Abraham.

In the earlier quoted Galatians 3:13, we saw that the death of Jesus "on a tree" (the wooden cross) redeemed those of us who have been born again from the curse *of the law,* and extends to us the Abrahamic blessing. But what about **the** curse, that is, the original curse which fell in the Garden of Eden? Did Jesus release us from that curse as well? Let me begin to answer these questions by establishing that God often deals with His people in stages. We see this pattern throughout Scripture. We might like to shorten these lengthy processes to a single instant of time. But for whatever reason, the Lord in His infinite wisdom usually chooses to accomplish His divine agenda in steps.

Even our salvation from sin and its ravages takes place in phases. Those of us who have been born again *are* saved, *are being* saved, and *will be* saved. I Corinthians 1:30 breaks down the 3 steps in this process as follows: "...you are in Christ Jesus, who has become for us wisdom from God -- that is, our [#1]* righteousness, [#2]* holiness and [#3]* redemption."

Our spirits (the eternal part of us which came from God) *have been saved* since the moment we surrendered our lives to Jesus Christ in repentance and faith. That's the instant our spirits were made <u>righteous</u>. Our souls (essentially our minds) *are being saved* through the process called sanctification, by which we are progressively set apart from sin and this current world system, and made <u>holy</u> unto the Lord. Finally, our bodies *will one day be saved* when Jesus returns to earth and those mortal bodies will then be <u>redeemed</u> as we receive glorified, or heavenly bodies like the one He had after His resurrection. Note that in a scriptural passage quoted earlier in this chapter (I Corinthians 15:49), it says "so *shall* we bear the likeness of the man from heaven," referring to that transformation in the *future* tense. After foretelling in the 21st chapter of Luke the dreadful events leading to His return, Christ encouraged His followers by instructing them: "When these things begin to take place, stand up and lift up your heads, because your *redemption* is drawing near." (Luke 21:28)

Galatians 3:13 presents our deliverance from the *curse of the law* in the past tense. It is from God's perspective an accomplished fact. But the *Edenic curse* is yet to be fully lifted. All human beings eventually die. Women still suffer intense pain in childbirth. The ground yet produces weeds, thorns, and thistles. Violence among earth's creatures continues to abound. And the process of decay rolls on unabated. But *our* full redemption and that *of the universe* are inextricably linked. Just as all those individuals redeemed through Christ Jesus will someday be fully freed from **the** curse, so will the rest of creation.

Listen to how the Apostle Paul explains this in Romans 8:18-25: "I consider that our present sufferings are not worth comparing with the glory that will be revealed in us. The creation waits in eager expectation for the sons of God to be revealed. For the creation was subjected to frustration, not by its own choice, but by the will of the one who subjected it, in hope that the creation itself will be liberated from its bondage to decay and brought into the glorious freedom of the children of God. We know that the whole creation has been groaning as in the pains of childbirth right up to the present time. Not only so, but we ourselves, who have the firstfruits of the Spirit, groan inwardly as we await eagerly for our adoption as sons, the redemption of our bodies. For in this hope we were saved. But hope that is seen is no hope at all. Who hopes for what he already has? But if we hope for what we do not have, we wait for it patiently." I'll address this subject of the final release from the Edenic curse in greater depth in the last chapter.

In connection with victory over this original curse, I need to remind you that in succumbing to Satan's devious temptation to sin and rebellion against God, Adam and Eve sold out us and the planet to the devil's dominion. Up until that moment, the first humans had been the Lord's children, and His representatives... exercising authority on earth on His behalf. From then on, the world system became the kingdom of Satan. Jesus Christ came to earth to wrest that kingdom from the slimy, oppressive grip of the devil, return it to it's rightful owner, allow a redeemed race of humans to become God's surrogates, and restore the creation to its original perfection.

But the price of that victory was to be measured in unthinkable agony and death. Before Jesus reached that decisive moment, Satan, as the god of this world, offered Him a phony shortcut. "...the devil took him to a very high mountain and showed him all the kingdoms of the world and their splendor. 'All this I will give you,' he said, 'if you will bow down and worship me.'" (Matthew 4:8,9) But our Savior would have no part of it. Jesus replied: "Away from me, Satan! For it is written" 'Worship the Lord your God, and serve him only.'" (Matthew 4:10)

Though He rebuffed the devil and the cheap pseudo route to victory he proffered, Jesus did not look forward to His sacrificial suffering and death. And it was not only the physical pain which concerned him, it was the absolute disgrace of sin that He would have to bear... the multiplied infamy of every sin of every sinner who *had* ever lived and who *would* ever live. Hebrews 12:2 advises us that it was His anticipation of the immense gratification He would experience upon redeeming all mankind that kept Him on course. "Let us fix our eyes on Jesus, the author and perfecter of our faith, who for the joy set before him endured the cross, scorning its shame…" On the eve of His crucifixion, as the bitter dregs of the toxic brew of sin approached His innocent lips, our Lord prayed in such aguish that the gospels note His sweat fell to the ground like "drops of blood." (Luke 22:44)

Luke 22:42 records His prayer in that awful hour: "Father, if you are willing, take this cup from me; yet not my will, but yours be done." The human side of Jesus apparently hoped for a last minute alternative from His Father, but determinedly committed Himself to accomplish the terrible task set before Him. The 2004 movie "The Passion of the Christ," produced by Mel Gibson, afforded hundreds of millions of people a remarkably graphic portrayal of the terrible physical suffering endured by Jesus Christ to purchase redemption for us. The price he paid in the currency of physical pain was horrific.

Yet I'm convinced that the greatest payment made by our Savior was not tendered through any bodily injury, though Roman crucifixion was known to be one of the most excruciating means of execution ever devised. The highest reparations for the crimes of all mankind were extracted from Jesus in that moment of what must have been absolute stark terror when He who had never sinned, bore the full effect of *our* sins. In that instant, in His absolute holiness, God the Father had to turn His back on sin. Then the Son of God who had previously known precious unbroken fellowship with His Father every second of His earthly life, screamed: "My God, My God, why have you forsaken me?" (Mark 15:34)

Only Jesus substitutionary death could reverse the curse and reclaim God's rightful jurisdiction over the dominions of this world. Only it could release us from thousands of years of Satan's malevolent reign. Paul rejoiced over this happy outcome in the opening lines of his letter to the churches in the region of Galatia. "Grace and peace to you from God our Father and the Lord Jesus Christ, who gave himself for our sins to rescue us from the present evil age..." (Galatians 1:3,4)

In the past several decades the expression "born again" has become part of popular American Christian culture. I've used it throughout this book. It's used by many people to describe a *certain kind* of Christian... a *born again* Christian. But according to the Bible no one can be a Christian at all without being born again. This phrase is also specifically linked to the destruction of the devil's kingdom on earth and the restoration of God's kingdom here.

In the 3rd chapter of the gospel of John, a Pharisee named Nicodemus came to speak with Jesus one night. We briefly referred to this encounter previously. Jesus told him: "...no one can see [perceive]* the kingdom of God unless he is born again." (John 3:3) Nicodemus was puzzled by this new expression, wondering aloud how a person could re-enter his mother's womb to be born a second time. So the Lord explained further: "Flesh gives birth to flesh, but the Spirit gives birth to spirit." (John 3:6) Jesus had not been speaking of another *physical* birth. Remember that Adam suffered *spiritual* death as well as physical death because of sin. When we in faith give our lives to the Lord, our dead spirits come to life through restored fellowship with God. At that moment we leave the kingdom of Satan, who rules over this present world system, and become part of the Lord's kingdom. In this era, God's kingdom is a spiritual one. But in an age yet to come, it will be a physical kingdom, too.

This was the primary purpose for which the Son of God came to us in human form. He did not just come to teach us a new way of life, He meant to destroy the power of the author (Satan) of the old way of life. He entered this sin-corrupted world to undo the curse. He intended to restore all that Adam and Eve had lost to the devil when they ate the forbidden fruit. In John 10:10, Jesus proclaimed: "The thief [Satan]* comes only to steal, kill and destroy; I have come that they may have life, and have it to the full." But for this present age that fullness of life has limits. Currently God's kingdom exists primarily in the spiritual dimension. Jesus told Pontius Pilate: "My kingdom is not of this world. If it were, my servants would fight to prevent my arrest by the Jews. But now my kingdom is from another place." (John 18:36)

Jesus understood that the effects of His work on earth would be implemented in stages, as described earlier in this chapter. There were earth-shattering events many centuries in the future which would precipitate the completion of God's plan of redemption. These events were to be incorporated into what is classified biblically as "the end times," or "the last days." One of the places Jesus spoke extensively of this period was in the 24th chapter of Matthew. After enumerating some of the happenings which would be the signs, or indicators, of the last days, He observed: "All these are the beginning of birth pains." (Matthew 24:8) Something new was to be *given birth* at the end of time. This is the same process later spoken of by Paul in the aforementioned Romans 8:22: "We know that the whole creation has been groaning as in the pains of childbirth right up to the present time." In the final chapter of this book, we'll catch an enticing glimpse of this *new* thing, which is in some ways an *old* thing.

*Not in the original text. Added by the author for clarification.

CHAPTER 8

The Curse Lifted

Have you ever watched a movie that drew your emotions into its plot so powerfully that you just had to see it through to the very finish? You wanted to witness love conquering all, good triumphing over evil, injustices made right, and insurmountable obstacles overcome. All through the film you endured the trials of the heroes and heroines with them, sharing their anguish and fear, their disappointments and tragedy... always anticipating the joy you'd feel when you got to that happy ending. But when the moment of truth finally arrived, it rudely slapped you across the face with a cruel twist! It left you not only heartbroken, but feeling cheated as well. I hate those kind of movies. How about you? Yet real life can be like that sometimes, too. Let me assure you that the real life story I've told you about in this book won't leave you with a stinging cheek and a broken heart. That's because it's based on the Word of God, and the Word of God promises a happy ending for those who trust in Him.

Let's begin this look at the Bible's happy ending with a closer examination of the release of God's people from the full effects of the curse. I previously revealed that this liberation occurs in phases. I stated that our *spirits* are saved from sin and the curse the moment we surrender our lives in faith to Jesus Christ. Our *souls* then enter the process of being saved. But our *bodies* will not be saved until a future time. Let me expand upon that fact a little more at this point.

It's a fact that through the death and resurrection of Jesus Christ the final victory over the Edenic curse of sin has been established. When we personally accept this salvation God provided through His Son, Jesus, our sins are forgiven, our spirits are transformed by the Spirit of God and we're saved. According to II Corinthians 5:17 we become a "new creation." Having been reconciled to the Lord, we become what He intended from the beginning for humans to be: God's very own children. This is what the Scripture refers to as being "born again." In describing this experience to the Jewish leader Nicodemus, Jesus made it clear that being born again occurred in the realm of the *spirit.* John 3:6 quotes Him as saying: "Flesh give birth to flesh, but the Spirit gives birth to spirit."

Once we receive this spiritual salvation through Jesus, our souls, still marred by the curse, embark on a lifelong progression through which we're being sanctified, or "set apart" *from* sin and *unto* God. As we press forward during this journey we draw slowly but steadily closer to the Lord, and grow in faith and righteousness. We may stumble many times, but by the grace of God we can always get up and get back on track. In this life we're being perfected into the likeness of our Savior and Elder Brother, Jesus.

The "sanctification" or "perfection" of the soul will be consummated at the moment of our physical death, as we view the Lord in His fullness and are fully changed into His perfect spiritual and moral image. At death our souls leave our bodies and enter the very presence of the Lord. The Apostle Paul expresses his desire for this escape from a sin cursed environment when he tells the Corinthian church: "We… would prefer to be away from the body and at home with the Lord." (II Corinthians 5:8)

But until that time, we are a work in progress. Paul puts it this way in II Corinthians 3:18: "And we, who… reflect [or contemplate]* the Lord's glory, are being transformed into his likeness with ever increasing glory, which comes from the Lord, who is the Spirit." Incidentally, a literal rendering of the original Greek for the phrase "with ever increasing glory" further confirms the *step by step* nature of God's work in the lives of those of us who have been born again. It literally reads: "from *glory* to *glory.*"

Through His prayer, noted in John chapter 17, Jesus Himself specified God's Word, enlightened by His Spirit, as the primary instrument of the aforementioned "reflection" or "contemplation" which accomplishes this transformation. As he prayed for His followers, He asked His Father to: "Sanctify them by the truth; your word is truth." (John 17:17) Though sanctification is a work of the Lord, it requires our active participation in reading, studying, and reflecting, contemplating, or meditating on the Scriptures.

Still, the limitations of this life apply for the present. "Now we see but a poor reflection as in a mirror; then we shall see face to face. Now I know in part; then I shall know fully, even as I am fully known." (I Corinthians 13:12) The Apostle John declared that the completion of our deliverance from the old human nature, corrupted by the curse, happens in that moment when we pass from this life and view Jesus unhindered by earthly restraints. He puts it this way: "…we shall be like him, for we shall see him as he is." (I John 3:2) That will be the final fulfillment of the wonderful promise Jesus made in Matthew 5:6: "Blessed are those who hunger and thirst for righteousness, for they will be filled."

While our *souls* will be fully released from the curse at the moment of death, our *bodies* will experience their final freedom at the resurrection of the righteous dead, when Jesus returns to earth. In that instant the bodies of born again believers, both those alive at His second coming and those already dead, will be reconstructed. The New Testament speaks of this in numerous places. I Thessalonians 4:16,17 offers one of the most well known descriptions of this fantastic event. "For the Lord himself will come down from heaven, with a loud command, with the voice of the archangel and with the trumpet call of God, and the dead in Christ will rise first. After that, we who are still alive and are left will be caught up together with them in the clouds to meet the Lord in the air. And so we will be with the Lord forever." In Philippians 3:20,21 we read: "And we eagerly await a Savior… the Lord Jesus Christ, who by the power that enables him to bring everything under his control, will transform our lowly bodies so that they will be like his glorious body." That's why Christians sometimes refer to the result of this future physical transformation as our "glorified bodies."

In I Corinthians 15:51-53 Paul again addresses the mysterious future conversion of our bodies. "…We will all be changed -- in a flash, in the twinkling of an eye, at the last trumpet. For the trumpet will sound, the dead will be raised imperishable, and we will be changed. For the perishable must clothe itself with the imperishable, and the mortal with immortality." In that moment, the bodies which have for millennia been in bondage to decay because of the curse, will become incorruptible. These re-made bodies will not be subject to sickness, pain, aging, or death. At this point, the deliverance of God's redeemed people from the Edenic curse will have been completed. But what about the rest of creation?

I began this book with truths from the first book of the Bible: Genesis. I now end it with facts from the last book of the Bible: Revelation. Both have been sneered at by skeptics. Each contains truths essential to adequately understanding the plan of God from beginning to end. Revelation in particular is often shied away from, even by Christian believers. This is largely due to the alarming nature of its discussion of end time events, and the difficulties encountered in comprehending its relatively eccentric and often symbolic text.

I will not be dealing with most of the contents of this closing book of the New Testament. I'll be concentrating on portions of its final three chapters as they relate to our subject: *the curse*. For those of you who have already committed your lives in faith to Jesus Christ, the truths in the last chapter of this book will fill you with wondrous and joyful anticipation. For those of you who have not yet received the Lord's salvation through Jesus, you'll catch a glimpse of the ultimate divine reconciliation of all those things presently out of order. Whether you participate in those blessed end time events, or suffer the eternal consequences of the curse will be up to you.

One of the primary keys to the deliverance of the earth

from the curse is the transfer of governmental control of the world back to God. Let me remind you that when Adam and Eve sinned, since they were God's ruling representatives on the planet, they sold us out to the authority of Satan. He became in effect, the god of this world. As the Last Adam, Jesus came to redeem us from the curse and buy back the planet and its people from the devil's control. Though tempted by Satan, as was the first Adam, Jesus (the Last Adam) never joined the devil's rebellion by committing sin, but always obeyed His Heavenly Father. Then by bearing our punishment in His own body on the cross, He took away the sins of the first Adam and all of his descendents who would choose by faith return to the Creator.

So through His substitutionary death and resurrection, Christ regained for Himself and all of His spiritual descendents the privilege to rule on earth as God's rightful heirs. Philippians 2:8-11 tells us that it was His humility and obedience to the point of crucifixion that qualified Jesus to receive this authority. "And being found in appearance as a man, he humbled himself and became obedient to death -- even death on a cross! Therefore God exalted him to the highest place and gave him the name that is above every name, that at the name of Jesus every knee should bow, in heaven and on earth and under the earth, and every tongue confess that Jesus Christ is Lord, to the glory of God the Father."

The force with which God the Father raised Jesus from the dead is the same power through which we will share in His divine authority. It was the Apostle Paul's prayer that the Christians in the ancient city of Ephesus understand this principle. "I pray also that the eyes of your heart may be enlightened in order that you may know the hope to which he has called you, the riches of his glorious inheritance in the saints [all born again believers]*, and his incomparably great power for us who believe. That power is like the working of his mighty strength, which he exerted in Christ when he raised him from the dead and seated him at his right hand in the heavenly realms, far above all rule and authority, power and dominion, and every title that can be given, not only in the present age but also in the one to come." (Ephesians 1:18-21) That's why the Scriptures are also able to declare that those who have been born again will one day rule and reign with Him. (II Timothy 2:12, Revelation 5:10) This aspect of God's plan for the ages through Jesus is, according to Ephesians 1:10: "...to be put into effect when the times will have reached their fulfillment -- to bring all things in heaven and on earth together under one head, even Christ."

The end time events described in the book of Revelation bring us to that magnificent future period. Once again we see that though God frequently *establishes* momentous things in a short space of time, their *implementation* often occurs in incremental steps, with the ultimate fulfillment arriving at a much later date. In Revelation 11:15 we can find ourselves standing with John at the sounding of the last of 7 apocalyptic trumpets at the end of time, after which he hears loud voices in heaven saying: "The kingdom of this world has become the kingdom of our Lord and of his Christ, and He will reign for ever and ever." At that prophetic moment the way is being prepared for the final revocation of the curse.

The scenes presented in chapters 20, 21, and 22 of Revelation take place during and after a thousand year reign of Christ on earth (commonly referred to as the *millennium*), during which Satan is chained in a place called "the Abyss." (Revelation 20:1) The resolution of divine righteousness follows on the heels of a final battle between the forces of good and evil, and the ensuing judgment of the unrighteous. At the close of the millennium, just prior to this judgment, Satan is released from his imprisonment, rallies nations of earth to his side through deception (always his modus operandi), and prepares them for battle against the Lord and His people. But fire from heaven destroys the sinful rebels, and the devil then receives his ultimate punishment at the hands of God.

As God appears on His great white throne to judge the human race, we're told "earth and sky" will flee from His presence. (Revelation 20:11). This is apparently the time spoken of by the Apostle Peter in II Peter 3:7 "…the present heavens and earth are reserved for fire, being kept for the day of judgment and destruction of ungodly men." Then he goes on to further describes that future event as follows: "The heavens will disappear with a roar; the elements will be destroyed by fire, and the earth and everything in it will be laid bare." (II Peter 3:10) Interestingly, in II Peter 3:6 the apostle had connected this impending end time event with the flood of Noah's day, citing both as examples of the certainty of God's judgment against sin. In Noah's time God judged the world by water, but he promised never to send a worldwide destructive flood again. So in the end time He will judge it by fire.

Immediately after the destruction of the *sin-cursed* earth and sky, all the ungodly men and women who ever lived are brought before God and judged. (Revelation 20:12-15) The books in which the Lord has detailed the behavior of every human being are opened, and their contents used to determine their punishment. Anyone whose name is not found written in *another* book, specifically identified as the "book of life," which contains the names of all who have been born again, is be cast into the "lake of fire." (Revelation 20:12) The book of Revelation repeatedly identifies this lake of fire as the "second death." (Revelation 2:11, 20:6, 20:14, 21:8) As I first explained in chapter 2 of this book, this second death is eternal separation from the God who loves us and prefers to bless us. But we as human beings are the ones who by our choice determine our own eternal destiny.

The context of the reference to the lake of fire further tells us that in this place of "burning sulfur" the devil and all his allies "will be tormented day and night for ever and ever." (Revelation 20:10) The judicial sentence to eternity in the lake of fire, which is the second death, applies to those who have rejected Christ and have been brought back to face final judgment. The foregoing events will bring one era to an end, and make way for the start of another. The era which concludes is the one in which we now live, which is under the curse. The passing of the old makes way for the new.

The Apostle John, the man who inspired by God penned the book of Revelation, introduces the new era as God had laid it before him in a supernatural vision of the future. It begins with Revelation 21:1. "Then I saw a new heaven and a new earth, for the first heaven and the first earth had passed away..." This fresh universe will be free of the corruptions of the curse. Revelation 21:2 goes on to record John's sighting of "the Holy City, the new Jerusalem." I'll touch on that topic a little more, later in this chapter. For now, let's ascertain what we can about the "new earth." The Bible as a whole, and Revelation in particular, do not provide many details concerning the new earth, but a few Bible passages give us some information.

The 11th chapter of the book of Isaiah begins with prophecies of the coming of Jesus, the Messiah. The references are to both His first appearance when He lived on earth, died, and rose from the dead for our salvation, and to His second advent when He will gather His people to Himself, then judge the earth. Following the prediction of His second coming to earth is a fascinating description of a mode of interaction among men and animals unknown to those of us who have lived under the curse. "The wolf will live with the lamb, the leopard will lie down with the goat, the calf and the lion and the yearling together; and a little child will lead them. The cow will feed with the bear, their young will lie down together, and the lion will eat straw like the ox. The infant will play near the hole of the cobra, and the young child put his hand into the viper's nest. They will neither harm nor destroy on all my holy mountain…" (Isaiah 11:6-9)

Such conditions clearly suggest those previously in effect on the earth in general, and specifically in the Garden of Eden, before the fall of mankind. Therefore, in a sense earth will have come full circle. The natural world at the end of time will be much like it was at the beginning. This restoration appears to be the future event referred to by the Apostle Peter in Acts 3:21. There he says of Jesus Christ: "He must remain in heaven until the time comes for God to restore everything…" The portrait of men and animals living at peace, painted by the above quoted passage from Isaiah 11:6-9, is but one of the many enchanting features of the newly recreated planet. Such changes are in a very powerful sense a "restoration" of the way God meant things to be from the beginning.

As with the original earth, the most delightful feature of the new earth will be the relationship of the Lord with His people. From his continuing glorious vision of the new epoch, John recalls for us: "And I heard a loud voice from the throne saying, 'Now the dwelling of God is with men, and he will live with them. They will be his people, and God himself will be with them and be their God.'" (Revelation 21:3) Here is suggested a virtual return to Eden which focuses on the primary reason why God made human beings in the first place.

A friend of mine once related to me an experience he had when he heard a preacher tell a congregation he was going to reveal to them in *one word* the Lord's purpose for the creation and redemption of mankind. My friend was pleased. He said he could forget a sermon. He could even fail to recall a sentence. But he knew he could remember *one word.* Then he told me: "Sam, when the preacher spoke that one word, I began to weep." That one word which revealed God's reason for creating people, and so deeply moved my friend was: ***fellowship***. God made us so that He and we might enjoy loving, intimate, and deeply satisfying fellowship. To be loved and desired is a wonderful thing. To be loved and desired by the God of the universe is beyond wonderful!

Anyone who has ever honestly contemplated the pleasures of life has come to the inevitable conclusion that nothing brings greater joy than relationships. People may seek fame, riches, achievements, or other emotional, ungodly type sexual, and chemical highs. But in the end, as they look back, the only enduring satisfaction they'll be able to take from their earthly lives will be drawn from the well of loving relationships. Counselors and confidants have disclosed the fact that as they approach the latter years of life, no successful business person has ever declared to them: "I wish I had spent more time at work!" Invariably, they regret not spending more time with their family. Wealthy is the person who dies in the caring arms of family and friends. Destitute is the one who breathes their last in the life-suffocating grip of selfish greed and ambition. We desperately need cherished love connections.

Personal rejection is one of the most difficult experiences in life. We *must* be loved and accepted. Human love, however, is quite fickle and frequently unreliable. God's love toward those who trust Him is an anchor of acceptance in what is often a turbulent sea of rejection. The grace of God which brings divine acceptance is available only through faith in Jesus Christ. "In love he [God]*... adopted us as sons through Jesus Christ, in accordance with his pleasure and will -- to the praise of his glorious grace, which he has freely given us in the One [Jesus]* he loves." (Ephesians 1:4-6) We who have been born again have already received this adoption. But its full endowment will only be realized in the future when "the dwelling of God is with men." (Revelation 21:3)

Loving human interaction is the supreme rank of earthly riches. But divine kinship is an even higher class of treasure. Israel's beloved King David exulted: "You [God]* have made known to me the path of life; you will fill me with joy in your presence, with eternal pleasures at your right hand." (Psalm 16:11) In some ways in this present existence it's easier to gain fulfillment from human fellowship, than from fellowship with God. Most of us are much more familiar with associations at the level of the soul and body. Though it calls to us from the depths of our being, the spiritual realm seems more distant and mysterious. But for those who respond to that remote longing, and seek and find the presence of God, we immediately realize nothing else in life compares to it.

The same David who, under the inspiration of the Holy Spirit of God penned the above quoted Psalm 16:11, later fell into terrible sin. When God confronted him with his wicked deeds through the ministry of a prophet named Nathan, he repented in profound godly sorrow. King David's prayer of repentance is found in Psalm 51. After pleading for forgiveness and cleansing from his sin, he feared great loss as a consequence of his transgressions. What was it that he was so afraid of losing? Was it his position as king? Was it the respect and love of his subjects? Was it his enormous wealth? The answer is found in Psalm 51:11 where he says to the Lord: "Do not cast me away from your presence or take your Holy Spirit from me." David valued fellowship with God more than anything else in life.

Even those of us who have enjoyed the presence of God in our lives here on earth, cannot entirely grasp the degree of blessed intimacy which will be ours in that new era described at the conclusion of the book of Revelation. The effects of the curse currently restrict the measure of, and subsequently the pleasure received from, our fellowship with the Lord. Relatively speaking, we've hardly even nibbled at an appetizer. In that day yet to come, I suspect the capacity of our relationship with God will not only be restored to that experienced by Adam and Eve in

Paradise, but will surpass it! The joy that awaits those who follow Jesus is literally unimaginable.

After the voice from the throne heard by John in Revelation chapter 21 speaks of the sweet fellowship awaiting us in the new creation, it goes on to tell of other wonderful changes as well. "'He [God]* will wipe every tear from their eyes. There will be no more death or mourning or crying or pain, for the old order of things has passed away.' He who was seated on the throne said, 'I am making everything new!'" (Revelation 21:4,5) The compassion of the Lord toward mankind is exhibited in His wiping "every tear from their eyes." Sometimes when we witness so many troubles, it's hard for us to remember that God is love and goodness. In the sorrows of life Satan whispers: "God doesn't care. If He did, this would never have happened." When we or others come under the judgment of a holy God for our disobedience, the devil insists: "God is just not fair!" We need to be reminded that these painful things were not meant by the Lord to be part of our existence. They entered our realm because the human race bought into Satan's lies and joined his unholy revolt against the Sovereign of the universe.

Even when God punishes sin, He still loves the sinner. In the Old Testament book of the prophet Ezekiel, the Lord bares His heart on this issue. "'Do I take any pleasure in the death of the wicked?' declares the Sovereign Lord. 'Rather, am I not pleased when they turn from their ways and live?'" (Ezekiel 18:23) "'For I take no pleasure in the death of anyone,' declares the Sovereign Lord. 'Repent and live!'" (Ezekiel 18:32) We see this same attitude demonstrated in God's Son Jesus when, in Luke 13:34, He lovingly looks out over a city full of people headed for judgment. "O Jerusalem, Jerusalem, you who kill the prophets and stone those sent to you, how often I have longed to gather your children together, as a hen gathers her chicks under her wings, but you were not willing!" Later, His emotions spilled over as He approached the city and lamented the spiritual blindness of His people. "If you, even you, had only known on this day what would bring you peace -- but now it is hidden from your eyes." (Luke 19:42)

In the end time scene here in the book of Revelation, God not only wipes away the tears of the people, He banishes the *origin* of their weeping. "The old order of things has passed away" and the Lord is "making everything new." He declares that in the *new* order "there will be no more death or mourning or crying or pain." (Revelation 21:4,5) In one stroke God eliminates the primary sources of sorrow: *pain and death*. The Greek word here translated "pain" is from the root word meaning "to toil for daily sustenance," and by implication refers to the pain that is the outcome of such toil. Thus, although I believe it also speaks of the distress of physical sickness and injury, and the pain of emotional hurt, it primarily means the anguish of painful hard labor.

Of course, such arduous toil is a consequence of the curse. God sentenced Adam and all his progeny to hard labor for his disobedience. "Cursed is the ground because of you; through painful toil you will eat of it all the days of your life... By the sweat of your brow you will eat your food until you return to the ground..." (Genesis 3:17,19) We may have important responsibilities in the life to come, but they will be the kind that bring joy, *not* grief.

Grief is the operative word when it comes to one of

pain's foremost comrades at arms: death. What in this present world brings deeper anguish than death? Death is the final blow. It is the chief sentence for the crime of sin. God had forewarned Adam and Eve of this consequence. "And the LORD God commanded the man, 'You are free to eat from any tree in the garden; but you must not eat from the tree of the knowledge of good and evil, for when you eat of it you will surely die.'" (Genesis 2:16,17) According to Romans 5:14 the fall of man allowed death to ascend to the throne: "...death reigned from the time of Adam..." We have all suffered from the loss of those dear to us. That separation from those whom we love is a most painful emotional experience. And we ourselves will die some day as well. These facts are a great blight upon life on our planet.

Death is an enemy to both God and man. In fact, it's classified as the *final* enemy. In I Corinthians 15:26 the Apostle Paul says: "The *last* enemy to be destroyed is death." If the first Adam paved the way for death to take control, then the Last Adam (Jesus) toppled death from its throne by rising from the dead. Later in that same chapter of I Corinthians, Paul makes this clear. At the conclusion of his discussion of death and resurrection, he invites us to rejoice with him in that triumph over death: "But thanks be to God! He gives us the victory through our Lord Jesus Christ." (I Corinthians 15:57)

Through original sin the devil once held the power of death (Hebrews 2:14), but by means of our Savior we have been effectively released from its fear and bondage. In Revelation 1:17,18 Jesus identifies Himself to a frightened Apostle John with these words of reassurance: "Do not be afraid. I am the First and the Last. I am the Living One; I was dead, and behold I am alive forever and ever! And I hold the keys of death and Hades [Hell]*."

In Revelation 21:4 we encounter the culmination of Jesus' conquest over our dreadful enemy as He proclaims "…there will be no more death." What an incredible moment that will be! Think of it. Never again will the breath of life that comes from God Himself depart and leave any living creature a motionless corpse. No more must we stand and grieve at the grave of a dearly departed. Sorrowful goodbyes will be a thing of the dark and distant past. Loving relationships will truly be *forever.* Even our friends, the animals, will never die. Feel the excitement with me as we stand in the presence of the Almighty and hear him in essence command: "Death, be gone forevermore!" A truly new dimension of our existence will have dawned.

Now let's turn our attention to the arrival of the new Jerusalem. To better understand the *new* Jerusalem, we must begin by distinguishing the essential significance of the *old* Jerusalem. The Bible uses various additional words and phrases as synonyms for Jerusalem. Some of the most common are: Zion (that is Mount Zion, upon which the city is built), the City of David, the City of God, and the Holy City. Jerusalem is first mentioned in Joshua 10:1 as a city of a group of pagan Canaanites. But it only took on significance to the Lord and His people after King David captured it (II Samuel 5:6-9) and brought the Ark of the Covenant (which represented the presence of God) into it (II Samuel 6:12).

Because of David's heart for God, the placing of God's symbolic "earthly dwelling" (Ark of the Covenant) there, and later the building of the Temple which housed the Ark of the Covenant, Jerusalem became special to the

Lord. The city and its inhabitants were deeply loved by Him. But over the centuries Jerusalem turned away from the Lord, and was eventually given over to destruction by the Romans in 70 A.D. It has since been rebuilt and will be the focus of the final confrontation between God and Satan. (Revelation 20:7-9)

But the old Jerusalem will be destroyed once and for all, along with the old heaven and earth, at the final judgment. The new Jerusalem will be a perfected version of the old, fully representing the Lord's presence among men. It's prophetically seen by John "coming down out of heaven from God." (Revelation 21:2) The new Jerusalem does not arrive at earth until this future instance, but it already exists in heaven. In Galatians chapter 4 Paul identifies the old Jerusalem with the Siniatic covenant, and with bondage to the law which we have all been incapable of fully keeping. In verse 26 he concludes: "But the Jerusalem that is above is free, and she is our mother."

Hebrews 12:22 indicates that in a spiritual sense we are already there. Speaking to believers in Christ, it says: "But you have come to Mount Zion, to the heavenly Jerusalem, the city of the living God." This is the metropolis which even the Old Testament believers joyously anticipated. Citing Abraham as the first example of such saints, Hebrews 11:10 tells us: "For he was looking forward to the city with foundations, whose architect and builder is God." New Testament (or born again) believers possess this same hope. "But our citizenship is in heaven." (Philippians 3:20)

The description of this city can overwhelm our imaginations. It starts in Revelation 21:10. John recounts: "And he [an angel]* carried me away in the Spirit to a mountain great and high, and showed me the Holy City,

Jerusalem, coming down out of heaven from God." And it ends with Revelation 22:5. "There will be no more night. They will not need the light of a lamp or the light of the sun, for the Lord God will give them light. And they will reign for ever and ever." I will touch on only a few of the details in between these verses… particularly those most pertinent to our subject. But you can read the entire narrative for yourself.

As with much of the contents of the book of Revelation, not every aspect of the truth is revealed, and complete and certain interpretation of the truths which are given is somewhat problematic. I won't attempt to suggest answers for every question arising from the Scriptural account, only the most compelling. The first uncertainty we encounter regarding the new Jerusalem is its precise final destination. We're specifically told where it comes from: heaven. But the account does not actually say whether the Holy City lands on the earth or if it comes to rest somewhere in proximity… perhaps in orbit around the planet. The exact point of its ultimate location is not specified.

The city's dimensions are listed as 12,000 stadia in length, width, and height. Converting this ancient measurement to miles gives us three dimensions of approximately 1,400 miles each. Most Bible scholars believe that this classifies the structure of the city as a cube, although a few think that it may be a pyramid. In either case it would be massive. The size of the new earth is not given. The initial presumption might be that it will be the same shape and size as the old, but we cannot know for sure.

Under current laws of physics, a structure the size of

the new Jerusalem resting at some place on the planet would generate catastrophe. However; we are not certain that the same laws of physics in force now will apply in the new universe. We're informed that the city will be accessible to the earth and its inhabitants (Revelation 21:24-27). But that does not necessarily argue for its location *on* the new earth. As I suggested earlier, it's possible that it may end up in orbit around the planet. It may even become something of a replacement for our present moon. Only God knows for certain. We are told that the city will have no need of the light of the sun and moon. (Revelation 21:23) Whatever the specific physical state of things, the new Jerusalem and the new earth will have a synergistic relationship, with God lovingly but absolutely ruling from His throne in the city.

There will be no need for a temple of worship in the new Jerusalem as there once was in the old Jerusalem. John says: "I did not see a temple in the city, because the Lord God Almighty and the Lamb [Jesus]* are its temple." (Revelation 21:22) The temple built in the old Jerusalem by King Solomon, was patterned after the tabernacle in the wilderness. The detailed design for that tabernacle was given by God to Moses on Mount Sinai during the wilderness journey of the Israelites from Egypt to the Promised Land. Each part of that structure represented some feature of the Lord's relationship to his people. But Hebrews 8:5 identifies that tabernacle as "a copy and shadow of what is in heaven." And Hebrews 8:2 refers to the site of Jesus' throne as "the true tabernacle set up by the Lord, not by man." It is through the arrival of this "true tabernacle," the new Jerusalem, that God's people will experience the reality of His end time edict: "Now the

dwelling of God is with men, and he will live with them."
(Revelation 21:3)

As I draw to the close of our discussion of the curse, I
call your attention to three relevant details in the account of
the new Jerusalem: the return of the tree of life, the lifting
of the curse, and the restoration of unfettered relationship
between God and His people.

Chapter 22 commences with these words: "Then the
angel showed me the river of the water of life, as clear as
crystal, flowing from the throne of God and of the Lamb
down the middle of the great street of the city. On each
side of the river stood the tree of life, bearing twelve crops
of fruit, yielding its fruit every month. And the leaves of the
tree are for the healing of the nations." (Revelation 22:1,2)
The existence of this "water of life" had first been revealed
by Jesus Himself while He lived and walked on earth. The
same John who penned the book of Revelation, recorded
the story of Jesus' encounter with a woman of Samaria
in the 4th chapter of his gospel. There the Christ offered
her an amazing beverage. He asserted that whoever
drank of the living water He gave, would find that it would
"become in him a spring of water welling up to eternal life."
(John 4:14) As quoted above, Revelation reveals that the
pure water of this river, which becomes a spring within
individuals, flows from the throne of God and of His Son.
And it is this same water which nourishes the "tree of life."
(Revelation 22:2)

You'll remember that this tree of life, which was once
in ancient Paradise, is the one to which Adam and Eve
and all of their descendents were denied access after they
joined Satan's rebellion. It was the loss of its fruit which
assured their and our deaths. (Genesis 3:22) No one in

recorded history since the departure of Adam and Eve has ever seen the Garden of Eden or the tree of life. But we are told in Revelation 22:2 that upon the arrival of the New Jerusalem at the end of time, the tree of life resides in that heavenly home.

Could it be that the entire Garden of Eden itself was long ago transplanted to heaven? In Revelation 2:7, the Spirit of God proclaims: "To him who overcomes, I will give the right to eat from the tree of life, which is in the Paradise of God." As noted before, Eden has also been referred to as Paradise. Whatever the details of the transition of the Garden of Eden and its tree of life over the centuries may be, this much is clear: here now in the new Jerusalem, is the tree whose fruit provides eternal life, irrigated by the river whose water gives eternal life. Death has been banished and humans may freely partake of the fruit of the tree of life.

But there are characteristics of the tree of life revealed in this vision of the city of God, which are new to us. John notes that there are a dozen "crops" or kinds of fruit borne by the tree. We're further told that it will yield fruit every month, presumably meaning that it produces fruit not just during certain earthly seasons, but continuously. Finally, it's said that the tree's *leaves* are "for the healing of the nations." (Revelation 22:2) The primary meaning of the Greek word rendered "healing" is: to serve, care for, or give attention to. It's the Greek word from which our English word *therapy* is derived. Some scholars believe that a better translation of the word in this context is "health." That it's leaves are for the health of the *nations* lets us know that the tree of life is accessible not only to those who live in the new Jerusalem, but to all the inhabitants of the new earth as well.

The first brief sentence of Revelation 22:3 brings a welcome end to the core topic of this book: "No longer will there be any curse." A somewhat awkward, but more literal rendering of the original Greek is: "And every curse will not be longer." The point is, not only will **the** curse of Genesis chapter 3 be abolished, but *every* curse ever brought upon mankind by our sin and disobedience will be banished forever! Gone evermore is the curse that drove Cain from the presence of the Lord, the curse on the planet delivered through the worldwide flood, the curses for disobedience of the law of Moses, and every curse that ever was. Sin has been dealt with once and for all, and only the *blessing* of God remains. The love, joy, and peace that we have all sensed were meant to be characteristic of life, have returned to the world!

Revelation 22:4 declares of the servants of God: "They will see his face, and his name will be on their foreheads." This unobstructed, undiminished view of the Lord's face speaks of a pure, intimate relationship between God and humans, untarnished by sin and rebellion. Because of God's holiness and our cursed sinfulness, the Bible repeatedly tells us that in this present realm no man can see God and survive the awful experience. In the glorious future realm, our experience of viewing the Almighty will be constant and exhilarating. The reconciling death of the only Savior of the world, Jesus Christ, has made it possible. Have you ever had moments where you and a loved one looked deeply into one another's faces and felt the nearly inexpressible delight of love? That would present a tiny foretaste of what lays ahead for those who serve God.

The significance of having His name on our *foreheads* should not be overlooked. There are several instances in the Old Testament where God marks, seals, and protects His own people through some kind of identification on their foreheads. The forehead is a most obvious place for an identifying mark. This shows that God will not be ashamed for anyone in the universe to see that we are His. Sin brought shame to both man and his Maker. But sin is now gone and the Lord is pleased to call us *His very own*. And we will be pleased to call Him *our God*. Again I proclaim, my friends, relationships are the most precious things in life. And the most precious relationship of all is the one with our Creator God. That fellowship will be the most distinguishing characteristic of life in the recreated universe.

Verses 7 and 12-14 of Revelation chapter 22 promise a *blessing*, not a *curse*, to all true believers. These believers, regardless of earthly denominational affiliations, comprise the Church or Body of Jesus Christ. Each of these passages cited above begins with the declaration of the Lord's soon return. The first goes on to declare blessing to the Church on the basis of its keeping (or preserving) the words of the prophecies in the book of Revelation. The second declaration follows the promise of the second coming with the statement: "Blessed are those who wash their robes, that they may have the right to the tree of life and may go through the gates into the city." (Revelation 22:14) Has your robe been washed clean in the blood of Jesus? Have you been born again? Then you are an heir to the *blessing* and not the *curse*!

From Genesis chapter 3 to Revelation chapters 20 through 22, life on earth has swung full circle. I've traced the journey from the blessings of God in the original creation, to the curses of sin in the present world, to the renewed divine blessings of the world to come. Are you weary to the bone with the troubles of this life? Join me and all who have surrendered themselves to God by faith in His plan of redemption through Jesus. And some wonderful day we shall all bid a jubilant "good riddance" to: *the curse!*

*Not in the original text. Added by the author for clarification.

CONCLUSION

Has life in this world disillusioned you? Has the suffering you've seen and experienced left you deeply troubled? Have you longed for something or someone to help you understand, and to overcome your fears? It's my prayer that this book has pointed you to the One who can bring clarity and peace to your troubled life. A songwriter put it this way:

In a world that often makes no sense,
Where misfortune sings its sad laments,
And a thousand voices all profess,
To offer truth and happiness,
There is only One I see,
He's the Rock unchanged eternally,
The anchor of my soul, His name is Jesus!

He remains faithful,
When the storms of doubt rain down their fears,
And the strong winds of confusion spin my weary mind.
He remains faithful,
He's the Rock of Ages ever near,
Master of the storm, He speaks and peace I find.
Even when my faith is small,

And I falter, He's still standing tall.
No matter where life's journeys go,
They lead me back to what I know:
He remains faithful.

As I conclude this book, I trust I've communicated enough truth to bring you crucial insights concerning these weighty matters. No human being can fully comprehend everything while in this realm. The Apostle Paul admitted in I Timothy 3:16: "Beyond all question, the mystery of godliness is great..." But enough can be known to bring us spiritual freedom. Jesus declared: "...you will know the truth, and the truth will set you free." (John 8:32) Knowing the essential facts about the curse of sin which introduced chaos into God's once perfect creation, and accepting by faith the accomplishments of the Son of God who came to redeem us from sin and the curse, *can* set us free.

I can verify this reality not only by the information shared in this volume, but from personal experience. I have spent more than five decades exploring and testing the veracity of the Bible. Though I do not have *all* the answers, life has taught me the faithfulness of the Lord and the reliability of the Bible. My experience is not free of all trouble, but I have been able to discover His loving, active participation in my life. The longer I have lived, the more valuable and consistent the eternal Word of God has proved to be. And I am not alone in this conviction, there are countless millions who would echo my testimony. You, too, can become a Christian and share in this genuinely fulfilling relationship with the Lord. Even science has confirmed the positive effect of Christianity in the lives of those who would follow Jesus. A study cited in an article in the November 10, 2003 issue of Newsweek magazine showed that people who don't attend church die at an average age of 75, while those who attend church more than once a week live to an average age of 83!

Still, for the born again child of God, the blessings received through faith in Christ in this life are only a small initial deposit. The best is yet to come. At the end of this age, we'll enter the new heaven and earth, totally free from the dreadful effects of the curse. For eternity we'll enjoy the full blessing of God as it was always meant to be. But those who have rejected God's plan of salvation through Jesus will spend eternity separated from this loving God in a very real place called Hell. Hell was not made for human beings, but for Satan and his fellow fallen angels. Unfortunately, people who follow the devil's deceitful, rebellious ways will share his final destination.

God has planned something wonderful for us. In Matthew chapter 25 Jesus told His followers about the final judgment. At that time the Lord will say to those who are righteous: "Come, you who are blessed by my Father; take your inheritance, the kingdom prepared for you since the creation of the world." (Matthew 25:34) But then he will say to the unrighteous: "Depart from me, you who are cursed, into the eternal fire prepared for the devil and his angels." (Matthew25:41) Rejecting the Creator is accepting Satan as god, qualifying us for the same fate prepared for him and his fallen angels.

Although God has made a way of escape from the curse, He will not force us to take that route. In the end, our destiny is in our own hands. Your decision to accept or reject God's offer of salvation through His Son, Jesus, will determine the disposition of your eternity. Hear the challenge of Joshua to the people of Israel in Deuteronomy 30:19. The same choice is yours in this moment. "This day I call heaven and earth as witnesses against you that I have set before you life and death, blessings and curses. Now choose life..." Pray this simple prayer to God from your heart:

Dear God, I confess that I'm a sinner. I need your forgiveness. I believe Jesus Christ died for my sins. I believe He rose from the dead to conquer death for me. By faith I accept Jesus as my own personal Savior. From this day forward I turn away from my life of sin and will follow Him and live the rest of my life for You. I know I will someday live forever with You. Thank you for saving me. In Jesus' name I pray. Amen.

Congratulations! Welcome to the family of God! Now, if you don't already have one, get a Bible of your own and begin to read and study it daily. Start developing the regular habit of prayer. And if you don't already attend one, find and join a Bible-believing church. You'll need the spiritual leadership of a pastor and the encouraging fellowship of other believers to grow in your newly discovered faith. My prayers will be with you. May the Lord richly bless you as you begin the adventure of a lifelong walk with Him!

RECOMMENDED
FURTHER READING

Author's comments: *While there are other fine books available dealing with the following topics, this list is composed of those which I have personally read and can heartily recommend. I have added a brief descriptive comment after each.*

On the Existence of God and the Veracity of Scripture -

"I Don't Have Enough Faith to Be an Atheist," by Norman L. Geisler and Frank Turek, Crossway Books

The authors deal meticulously with all the major arguments against the existence of God and the authority and authenticity of the Bible, and present the powerful evidences and arguments which support of those beliefs. They respond not simply with religious rhetoric, but with philosophically sound, rational questions and answers. This book is only for those willing to honestly examine their belief system.

On Creation versus Evolution -

"In the Minds of Men," by Ian T. Taylor, TFE Publishing

This is a comprehensive, well-documented volume tracing the rise of the theory of evolution and its effect on the church and society at large, and revealing many of its past and present errors. It's nearly 500 pages require a slow and careful read at times because of the volume of information being conveyed, but that effort will be richly rewarded. This book is a terrific primer on the issue of evolution.

On the Worldwide Flood -

"The Genesis Flood," by Drs. John C. Whitcomb and Henry M. Morris, Baker Book House

A classic and thorough work, this document expounds upon the Bible account of the deluge, relating it to science and dealing intelligently with many of the secular and religious objections to the flood. Originally published in 1961, some of its content is a bit dated, but its nearly 500 pages of text are well worth the reading.

"The World That Perished," by Dr. John C. Whitcomb, Baker Book House

Written by one of the co-authors of "The Genesis Flood," this book is an updated, less technical, more succinct and readable follow up. It adds an entire section dealing with the issue of the Bible's veracity.

On the Pre-Flood Environment -

"Panorama of Creation," by Dr. Carl E. Baugh, Hearthstone Publishing

Dr. Baugh presents a rather unique treatment of this historical period, illuminating the wisdom of God demonstrated in the creation, while proposing a well thought out, fascinating theory about the pre-flood world.

On the Intelligence of Ancient Humans -

"The Puzzle of Ancient Man," by Dr. Donald E. Chittick, Creation Compass

Dr. Chittick deals with a wonderfully intriguing subject from the perspective of both the Bible and logical thought. This book cites information about many pertinent archeological discoveries and includes some illustrations and nice color photos of interest.

On the Nephilim -

"The Omega Conspiracy," by I.D.E. Thomas, Hearthstone Publishing

Though I may not necessarily agree with some of this book's conclusions, it is a detailed, well-documented look at the Nephilim, starting with the Scriptures, and supplementing it with numerous other credible historical sources of information.

<u>On all Matters of Life, Death, and Things Spiritual -</u>

"The Bible"

No other book on this list is so indispensable as the Holy Bible. Having spent most of my life studying its truths, I speak from significant experience. I do not yet fully understand every single word, phrase, and line of it, but I have absorbed and applied enough of it to vouch for its veracity and value on matters both spiritual and practical.

Printed in the United States
by Baker & Taylor Publisher Services